Get Grade

5

WJEC EDUQAS GCSE (9–1)

English Language

Richard Vardy

HODDER
EDUCATION
AN HACHETTE UK COMPANY

Orders: please contact Bookpoint Ltd, 130 Park Drive, Milton Park, Abingdon, Oxon OX14 4SE. Telephone: +44 (0)1235 827827. Fax: +44 (0)1235 400401. Email: education@bookpoint.co.uk Lines are open from 9 a.m. to 5 p.m., Monday to Saturday, with a 24-hour message answering service. You can also order through our website: www.hoddereducation.co.uk

ISBN: 978 1 5104 74246

© Richard Vardy 2020

First published in 2020 by

Hodder Education,

An Hachette UK Company

Carmelite House

50 Victoria Embankment

London EC4Y 0DZ

www.hoddereducation.co.uk

Impression number   10 9 8 7 6 5 4 3 2 1

Year   2024 2023 2022 2021 2020

Typeset by Integra Software Services Pvt. Ltd., Pondicherry, India

Printed in Spain

A catalogue record for this title is available from the British Library.

Contents

Introduction

How this workbook is structured

This revision workbook focuses on how to achieve a Grade 5 in your WJEC Eduqas GCSE English Language.

Chapter 2 provides you with an overview of the two exam components. There is also an opportunity for you to assess the current level of your skills so that you can ensure your revision is targeted on the areas that need it the most.

The subsequent chapters take you through the requirements of each question in the reading section of Component 1 and Component 2, followed by the requirements for the writing sections of Component 1 and Component 2.

As well as guidance, advice and carefully designed activities, you will also find extracts of student responses with accompanying commentaries. You will be able to see and explore the differences between a Grade 3 response and a Grade 5 response. There are spaces to write your answers throughout the workbook.

At the end of the workbook, there are two full sample exam papers, one for Component 1 and one for Component 2.

Key elements of this workbook
Overview of the question

Each chapter begins with a summary of what each question will ask you to do, how many marks it is worth and how long you should spend answering it.

> **Questions 1 and 3: Identifying explicit and implicit information and ideas**
>
> For Component 2, Questions 1 and 3 you will be asked to identify information in the texts. The answers may be explicit or implicit. You will just need to find short quotations or summarise what is clearly there.
>
> Question 1 will be on the first text (21st century). Question 3 will be on the second text (19th century). The questions will probably be broken down into smaller parts, such as a), b) and c).
>
> There are three marks for each of these two questions. Aim to spend about three to five minutes on each question.

Example exam question

Example exam questions for all sections are fully annotated with top tips and advice regarding the best ways to approach the question.

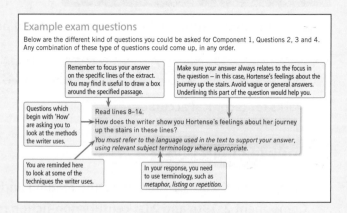

> **Example exam questions**
>
> Below are the different kind of questions you could be asked for Component 1, Questions 2, 3 and 4. Any combination of these type of questions could come up, in any order.
>
> Remember to focus your answer on the specific lines of the extract. You may find it useful to draw a box around the specified passage.
>
> Make sure your answer always relates to the focus in the question – in this case, Hortense's feelings about the journey up the stairs. Avoid vague or general answers. Underlining this part of the question would help you.
>
> Questions which begin with 'How' are asking you to look at the methods the writer uses.
>
> Read lines 8–14.
> How does the writer show you Hortense's feelings about her journey up the stairs in these lines?
> *You must refer to the language used in the text to support your answer, using relevant subject terminology where appropriate.*
>
> You are reminded here to look at some of the techniques the writer uses.
>
> In your response, you need to use terminology, such as *metaphor, listing* or *repetition*.

How do I achieve a Grade 5 in my response to this question?

This section provides you with a summary of the specific criteria of a Grade 5 response for the question.

> **How do I achieve a Grade 5 in my response to this task?**
>
> You will need to satisfy the following criteria in order to achieve a Grade 5 for the writing section of Component 1:
> - You need to communicate your ideas clearly and effectively.
> - Your writing needs to be clearly matched to the task you have chosen.
> - You need to use individual words, phrases and methods to impact your readers.
> - You will need to organise your whole piece of writing, and the paragraphs within it.

Activities and texts

To help you improve your responses, there are varied activities throughout this workbook all closely linked to exam questions and skills. They are designed to move you towards achieving a Grade 5 in GCSE English Language. The texts are typical of the types of texts you will encounter in the reading sections of your exams.

ACTIVITY 2

This extract is taken from Alexander Baron's novel From the City, From the Plough. *The novel tells the story of a group of soldiers as they prepare for D-day, an important battle in the Second World War.*

> The railway carriage was full of men and smoke and the smell of wet uniforms drying. Above each row of seats the space between luggage-rack and ceiling was jammed with packs and equipment. There were more packs piled in the corridor outside, and men squatting on them all along the corridor.
>
> 5 There was the noise of the train and of many men talking and laughing; and in the carriage the noise, wavering and mournful, of a mouthorgan.
>
> 'Put that bloody thing away,' said the sergeant who was sitting pressed tight against the window by the crush of bodies. He was watching the rain stream down the windowpane and he did not turn his head as he spoke.

Read lines 1–6.
List five things you learn about the railway carriage in these lines.

Exam tips

Throughout the workbook there are top tips and advice on the effective ways to achieve a Grade 5 in all sections and components of the exam.

EXAM TIP

Your reading and ideas for Questions 1–5 are good preparation for this question. By the time you get to Question 6, you should have a good understanding of both texts. Don't worry too much about repeating some points or quotations from previous responses: just make sure you are always answering the question.

Extended practice

Towards the end of each chapter, you are provided with a full sample exam question to answer under timed conditions. This is an invaluable opportunity to apply and demonstrate the skills covered in the chapter and to see the progress you have made towards achieving a Grade 5.

Extended practice

Complete the following Component 2 writing tasks. Limit yourself to one hour in total – 30 minutes on each task. Remember to carefully plan and structure each of your responses and to consider and apply the skills covered in this chapter.

Answer Question 1 **and** Question 2.
Think about the purpose and audience for your writing.
You should aim to write about 300–400 words for each task.

1 'Celebrities make good role models for young people.'
  You have been asked to contribute to a classroom debate on this topic. Write a speech in which you argue for or against the statement.

2 Write an engaging guide for visitors to your local area, advising them what to see and do.

Check your progress and Your reflections

Each chapter will conclude with a self-assessment exercise based on the Extended practice task. This will enable you to establish how confident you feel and to identify areas for further practice and consolidation.

CHECK YOUR PROGRESS

You have now practised the skills needed for a Grade 5 response to Component 2, Question 5. Read through your response to the Extended Practice task and identify where you have satisfied the criteria for a Grade 5. Complete the table by ticking the statements which apply to your response.

	✔
I wrote two paragraphs.	
I began each paragraph with an overview that summed up the point I was making.	
I selected evidence from both texts.	
The evidence I selected was relevant to the focus in the question ('the experiences and attitudes of lifeboat volunteers').	
I used comparative signposts such as 'both writers', 'similarly', 'on the other hand'.	

Your reflection
Are there any statements you did not tick? If so, how can you make sure you include these features in future responses?

....

....

....

....

A summary of the two exam papers

About Component 1: '20th Century Literature Reading and Creative Prose Writing'

This exam assesses your ability to read an extract from a 20th century fiction text. The exam also assesses your ability to write creatively. The exam lasts for 1 hour and 45 minutes and is split into two sections.

Section A: Reading

Question 1	This question will ask you to find five details from the text.	5 marks
Question 2	This question will ask you how the writer uses language for a particular effect, such as to establish character.	5 marks
Question 3	This question will either be another language question, or a question asking you what impressions you get of a character, event or place.	10 marks
Question 4	Depending on what you were asked for Question 3, this question will either ask you how the writer uses language for a particular effect or for your impressions of a character, event or place.	10 marks
Question 5	This question will either ask you whether you agree with a statement about the text or for you to evaluate the way someone or something is presented.	10 marks

Section B: Writing

You will choose one creative writing task from a choice of four.	40 marks

Managing your exam time for Component 1

Running out of time is a very common way for students to lose marks in their exam. You should plan your time to get the most out of every minute and avoid spending too long on one question. Listed below is an approximate outline of how you should plan your time for Component 1.

Component 1 is 1 hour 45 minutes long.

Read the text and the questions	10 minutes
Answer Question 1	5 minutes
Answer Question 2	5–7 minutes
Answer Question 3	10–12 minutes
Answer Question 4	10–12 minutes
Answer Question 5	10–15 minutes
Plan the response to the writing task	10 minutes
Complete the writing task	30 minutes
Check and proofread your response	5 minutes

About Component 2: '19th and 21st Century Non-Fiction Reading and Transactional/Persuasive Writing'

The exam assesses your ability to read and compare two texts. The texts will be on a linked subject and will be non-fiction (such as diaries, articles and biographies). One will be written in the 19th century and one will be written in the 21st century. The exam will also assess your ability to write for different purposes and audiences. The exam lasts 2 hours and is divided into two sections.

Section A: Reading

Question 1	This question will be divided into parts. You will have to find a detail from the first text for each part.	3 marks
Question 2	This question will ask you how the writer uses language and techniques for a particular purpose. It will be based on the first text.	10 marks
Question 3	This question will be similar to Question 1 but will be based on the second text. You will have to find specific details from the text.	3 marks
Question 4	This question will be based on the second text. It will ask you how successful you think the writer is in achieving a specific purpose, or how you think and feel about a particular aspect of the text.	10 marks
Question 5	This question will be on both texts and will ask you to find and combine short details and evidence.	4 marks
Question 6	This question will ask you to compare the attitudes of both texts and how they are presented.	10 marks

Section B: Writing

Question 1	These two tasks will assess your ability to write non-fiction texts for different audiences and purposes.	20 marks
Question 2		20 marks

Managing your exam time

Listed below is an approximate outline of how long you should spend on each question for Component 2.

Component 2 is 2 hours long.

Read the text and the questions	10 minutes
Answer Question 1	3–5 minutes
Answer Question 2	10–12 minutes
Answer Question 3	3–5 minutes
Answer Question 4	10–12 minutes
Answer Question 5	5 minutes
Answer Question 6	10–15 minutes
Plan the response to the first writing task	5 minutes
Complete the first writing task	20 minutes
Check and proofread your response to the first writing task	5 minutes
Plan the response to the second writing task	5 minutes
Complete the second writing task	20 minutes
Check and proofread your respond to the second writing task	5 minutes

Assessing your skills

When you revise, you should spend more time on skills you feel less confident about. Look back over the work you have completed over the last year, including any responses you have received feedback on. Note the questions and skills you found more challenging.

Then complete the table below. It includes the skills needed to get a Grade 5 for your GCSE English Language. You can then use the table to help you to prioritise your revision on the skills and questions you feel less confident about.

Reading							
Skill descriptor	**Question**	**Self-assessment (1 = struggling, 5 = very confident) ✔**					**Go to**
Identify and interpret information and ideas	C1 Q1 C2 Q1, 3	1	2	3	4	5	Page 10 Page 42
Select and synthesise (combine) evidence from two texts	C2 Q5	1	2	3	4	5	Page 68
Explain how writers use language and structure	C1 Q2, 3, 4 C2 Q2	1	2	3	4	5	Pages 10 and 15 Page 48
Evaluate a text by providing your own assessment	C1 Q5 C2 Q4	1	2	3	4	5	Page 33 Page 60
Compare how writers convey their ideas and perspectives	C2 Q6	1	2	3	4	5	Page 75
Use relevant subject terminology	C1 Q2, 3, 4, 5 C2 Q2, 4, 6	1	2	3	4	5	Pages 10, 15, and 33 Pages 48, 60, and 75
Support ideas with textual references and quotations	C1 Q2, 3, 4, 5 C2 Q2, 4, 5, 6	1	2	3	4	5	Pages 10, 15 and 33 Pages 48, 60, 68 and 75

Writing					
Skill descriptor	**Self-assessment (1 = struggling, 5 = very confident) ✔**				
Communicate clearly	1	2	3	4	5
Structure ideas together	1	2	3	4	5
Write in an appropriate style for the task	1	2	3	4	5
Write in full, accurate sentences with a range of punctuation	1	2	3	4	5
Spell most words accurately	1	2	3	4	5
Use a range of vocabulary and language devices to affect the reader	1	2	3	4	5

Component 1, Section A: 20th Century Literature Reading

Question 1: Identifying explicit and implicit information and ideas

For Component 1, Question 1 you will be asked to list five points you have found in the opening section of the text. The answers may be explicit (which means clear and obvious) or they may be implicit (which means you have to work out what the writer is suggesting).

The question is worth five marks. You should aim to spend about five minutes answering the question.

Example exam question

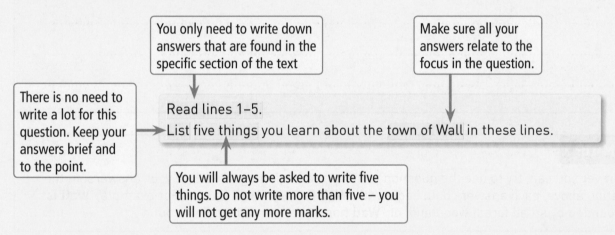

You only need to write down answers that are found in the specific section of the text

Make sure all your answers relate to the focus in the question.

There is no need to write a lot for this question. Keep your answers brief and to the point.

Read lines 1–5.
List five things you learn about the town of Wall in these lines.

You will always be asked to write five things. Do not write more than five – you will not get any more marks.

How do I achieve a Grade 5 in my response to this question?

The aim of this question is to allow you to get started and build some confidence in dealing with the text. You should follow these four steps to help you answer the question and ensure you get as many marks as possible.

1 Underline the key focus in the question. This will help you to ensure you are answering the question.
2 Draw a box around the section of text the question is asking you to consider. This will help to ensure all your answers are from the correct section.
3 Underline the words and phrases in the text that relate to the focus in the question.
4 Write your list in answer to the question. Try to summarise the piece of information, using your own words as much as possible. Avoid quoting whole sentences, word for word.

ACTIVITY 1

Complete Steps 1–4 for the question on *Stardust* printed below.

This extract is taken from the opening chapter of a fantasy novel by Neil Gaiman called Stardust.

> The town of Wall stands today as it has stood for six hundred years, on a high jut of granite amidst a small forest woodland. The houses of Wall are square and old, built of grey stone, with dark slate roofs and high chimneys; taking advantage of every inch of space on the rock, the houses lean into each other, are built one upon the next, with here and there a bush or tree growing out of the side of the building.

ACTIVITY 1

5 There is one road from Wall, a winding track rising sharply up from the forest, where it is lined with rocks and small stones. Followed far enough south, out of the forest, the track becomes a real road, paved with asphalt; followed further the road gets larger, is packed at all hours with cars and lorries rushing from city to city. Eventually the road takes you to London, but London is a whole night's drive from Wall.

Read lines 1–4.
List five things you learn about the town of Wall in these lines.

1 ....

2 ....

3 ....

4 ....

5 ....

EXAM TIP

Wherever you can, try to use the question focus at the beginning of each of your answers. In the question above, each answer could begin with 'Wall is ...' or 'Wall has ...'. For example, 'Wall is surrounded by small forest woodland' or 'Wall has only one road leading from it'.

ACTIVITY 2

This extract is taken from Alexander Baron's novel From the City, From the Plough. *The novel tells the story of a group of soldiers as they prepare for D-day, an important battle in the Second World War.*

The railway carriage was full of men and smoke and the smell of wet uniforms drying. Above each row of seats the space between luggage-rack and ceiling was jammed with packs and equipment. There were more packs piled in the corridor outside, and men squatting on them all along the corridor.

5 There was the noise of the train and of many men talking and laughing; and in the carriage the noise, wavering and mournful, of a mouthorgan.

'Put that bloody thing away,' said the sergeant who was sitting pressed tight against the window by the crush of bodies. He was watching the rain stream down the windowpane and he did not turn his head as he spoke.

Read lines 1–6.
List five things you learn about the railway carriage in these lines.

ACTIVITY 2

Read the extract from *From the City, From the Plough* above and the accompanying question. Then look at a student's answers to the question below. There is an error in each answer. In the space provided, explain the error you think the student has made. The first has been completed for you.

1 Rain was streaming down the windowpane.

This answer is wrong because the description of the rain is not in the section specified in the question.

2 The sound of the mouthorgan is mournful and wavering.

....

....

3 The railway carriage was full of men and smoke and the smell of wet uniforms drying.

....

....

4 There was an empty space above each row of seats.

....

....

5 The men in the railway carriage were silent.

....

....

Identifying implicit ideas

Writers do not always state their meaning obviously. Sometimes Question 1 will ask you to work out what the writer is suggesting or implying. This is sometimes referred to as reading between the lines.

The following extract is an early passage from The Silent Companions, *a novel by Laura Purcell.*

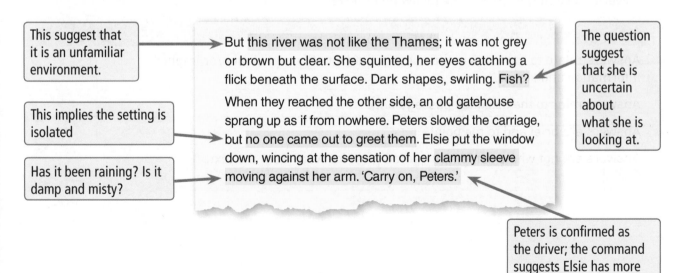

This suggest that it is an unfamiliar environment.

This implies the setting is isolated

Has it been raining? Is it damp and misty?

But this river was not like the Thames; it was not grey or brown but clear. She squinted, her eyes catching a flick beneath the surface. Dark shapes, swirling. Fish?

When they reached the other side, an old gatehouse sprang up as if from nowhere. Peters slowed the carriage, but no one came out to greet them. Elsie put the window down, wincing at the sensation of her clammy sleeve moving against her arm. 'Carry on, Peters.'

The question suggest that she is uncertain about what she is looking at.

Peters is confirmed as the driver; the command suggests Elsie has more authority.

Extended practice

Answer this Component 1, Question 1 example. After you have read the extract, limit yourself to five minutes, which is how long you should spend answering this question in the exam. Remember to consider and apply the skills and approaches covered in this chapter.

This extract is taken from the opening of a short story by V. S. Pritchett called 'The Fly in the Ointment'.

It was the dead hour of a November afternoon. Under the ceiling of level mud-coloured cloud, the latest office buildings of the city stood out alarmingly like new tombstones, among the mass of older buildings. And along the streets, the few cars and the few people appeared and disappeared slowly as if they were not following the roadway or the pavement but some inner, personal route. Along the road to the main
5 station, at intervals of two hundred yards or so, unemployed men and one or two beggars were dribbling slowly past the desert of public buildings to the next patch of shop fronts.

Presently a taxi stopped outside one of the underground stations and a man of thirty-five paid his fare and made off down one of the small streets.

'Better not arrive in a taxi,' he was thinking. 'The old man will wonder where I got the money.'

Read lines 1–6.
List five things you learn about the city in these lines.

1 ....

2 ....

3 ....

4 ....

5 ....

CHECK YOUR PROGRESS

You have now practised the skills needed for Component 1, Question 1. Read through your answers. Have they each met the following criteria?

	✔
Answers relate to the focus in the question and identify explicit and/or implicit information and ideas.	
Answers refer to the assigned passage only.	
Answers are brief and to the point.	
Answers are not whole sentences quoted word for word from the text.	

Questions 2, 3 and 4: Writing about language and structure

For Component 1, Questions 2, 3 and 4 you will be asked how the writer uses language for a particular purpose, such as to create suspense, to show the feelings of a character or to show a relationship between characters. Some questions might ask you what impression you get of a place, person or event in the text.

In some questions, you will also need to consider how the writer has structured the text. All three questions will direct you towards specific passages within the text. There is not a definitive order for these questions.

Question 2 is worth five marks and you should spend up to seven minutes answering it.

Questions 3 and 4 are each worth ten marks. You should spend up to 12 minutes answering each of these questions.

Example exam questions

Below are the different kind of questions you could be asked for Component 1, Questions 2, 3 and 4. Any combination of these type of questions could come up, in any order.

Remember to focus your answer on the specific lines of the extract. You may find it useful to draw a box around the specified passage.

Make sure your answer always relates to the focus in the question – in this case, Hortense's feelings about the journey up the stairs. Avoid vague or general answers. Underlining this part of the question would help you.

Questions which begin with 'How' are asking you to look at the methods the writer uses.

Read lines 8–14.

How does the writer show you Hortense's feelings about her journey up the stairs in these lines?

You must refer to the language used in the text to support your answer, using relevant subject terminology where appropriate.

You are reminded here to look at some of the techniques the writer uses.

In your response, you need to use terminology, such as *metaphor, listing* or *repetition*.

You may be provided with bullet points. Use these as prompts to help you as you write your answer.

Rather than a character or a place, some questions might ask you to analyse how an overall mood or atmosphere is created.

Read lines 8–14.

How does the writer create a sense of fear and dread in these lines?

You should write about:

■ what happens in these lines to create a sense of fear and dread
■ the writer's use of language and structure to create a sense of fear and dread
■ the effects on the reader.

You must refer to the text to support your answer using relevant subject terminology where appropriate.

Questions 3 and/or 4 may ask you to consider how the writer has structured the text as well as the language used. You could, for example, consider any significant changes in focus across the text, or any contrasts between characters.

You may be asked for your 'impression' of a text – this is asking you for *your* view.

Read lines 8–14.

What impressions do you get of the room in these lines?

You must refer to the text to support your answer using relevant subject terminology where appropriate.

How do I achieve a Grade 5 in my response to these questions?

These questions assess your ability to write about the effects of the way a writer has used language and structure. To get a Grade 5 response, you need to:

■ have a clear understanding of the text
■ explain clearly the effects of language and structure
■ select a range of relevant quotations and details from the text
■ use subject terminology appropriately and accurately.

Developing a clear understanding of the text

Before you answer the questions, you must make sure you have a good understanding of the text as a whole. This will assist you when you come to explain the effects of language and structure. Ask yourself the following questions:

■ What happens in the text?
■ What do we learn about the character(s) and/or place?
■ What do you think the writer is trying to achieve in the extract?

In order to develop a clear understanding of the text, you must read the text carefully all the way through. If you start answering the questions without this understanding, you will find it difficult to explain and analyse the effects of language and structure.

The following extract is an early passage from The Silent Companions, *a novel by Laura Purcell. Newly widowed Elsie has been sent to her late husband's country estate, called The Bridge. She is travelling with her cousin, Sarah.*

When they reached the other side, an old gatehouse sprang up as if from nowhere. Peters slowed the carriage, but no one came out to greet them. Elsie put the window down, wincing at the sensation of her clammy sleeve moving against her arm. 'Carry on, Peters.'

'There!' cried Sarah. 'The house is there.'

5 The road sloped down across a range of hills, where the sun was beginning to set. At the very end, crouching in a horseshoe of red and orange trees, was The Bridge.

Elsie put up her veil. She saw a low-slung **Jacobean building** with three gables on the roof, a central lantern tower and redbrick chimneys looming behind. Ivy poured out of the eaves and engulfed the turrets at either end of the house. It looked dead.

10 Everything was dead. **Parterres** lay prostrate beneath the soulless gaze of the windows, the hedges brown and riddled with holes. Vines choked the flowerbeds. Even the lawns were yellow and sparse, as if a contagion spread slowly throughout the grounds. Only the thistle thrived, its purple spikes bristling from amidst the coloured gravel.

The carriage drew to a halt on a gravel sweep, opposite the fountain that formed the centrepiece of the
15 decaying grounds. Once, when the stone was white and the sculpted figures of dogs on top were new, it must have been a handsome structure. No water sprang from the jets. Cracks wiggled across the empty basin.

Sarah drew back. 'They're all out to see us,' she said. 'The entire staff!'

20 Elsie's stomach plunged. She had been too busy staring at the gardens. Now she observed three women dressed in black waiting outside the house. Two wore white caps and aprons while the third was bare-headed, showing a coil of iron hair. Beside her stood a stiff, formal-looking man.

Elsie looked down at her skirts. They were patched like a rusty iron gate. Mud made the **bombazine** heavy and caused it to cling around her knees. What would her new servants think if they saw her in such a state? She would be neater and cleaner in her factory clothes.

Jacobean building: the house was built in a particular style common during the reign of King James I (1603–1625)

Parterres: a level garden used for ornamental flower beds

Bombazine: a type of fabric which was used in clothes worn by women in mourning

---

ACTIVITY 1

Read the extract above from *The Silent Companions*.

a) What happens in the text?

....

....

b) What do we learn about Elsie? Circle the statements which you think are true.

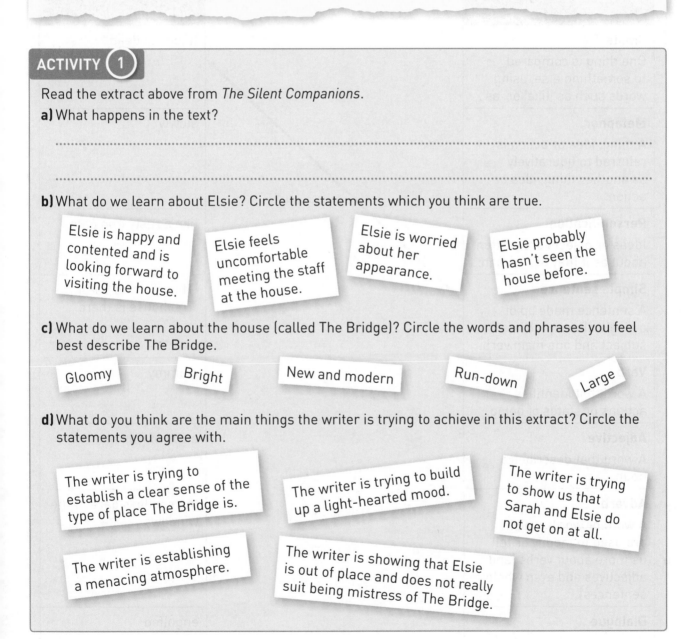

> Elsie is happy and contented and is looking forward to visiting the house.

> Elsie feels uncomfortable meeting the staff at the house.

> Elsie is worried about her appearance.

> Elsie probably hasn't seen the house before.

c) What do we learn about the house (called The Bridge)? Circle the words and phrases you feel best describe The Bridge.

> Gloomy

> Bright

> New and modern

> Run-down

> Large

d) What do you think are the main things the writer is trying to achieve in this extract? Circle the statements you agree with.

> The writer is trying to establish a clear sense of the type of place The Bridge is.

> The writer is trying to build up a light-hearted mood.

> The writer is trying to show us that Sarah and Elsie do not get on at all.

> The writer is establishing a menacing atmosphere.

> The writer is showing that Elsie is out of place and does not really suit being mistress of The Bridge.

Using subject terminology

In order to get a Grade 5, you must show that you can use subject terminology accurately.

EXAM TIP

Avoid 'feature spotting' in the exam. Only use subject terminology where it is appropriate to do so and when you can explain the effects of the technique.

ACTIVITY 2

Match the term with an example from the extract from *The Silent Companions*.

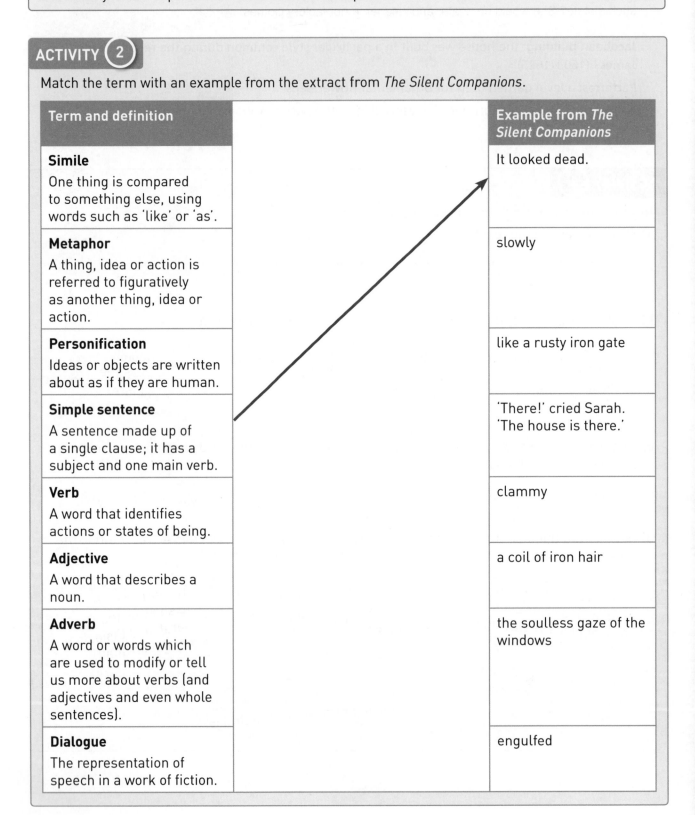

Term and definition		Example from *The Silent Companions*
Simile One thing is compared to something else, using words such as 'like' or 'as'.		It looked dead.
Metaphor A thing, idea or action is referred to figuratively as another thing, idea or action.		slowly
Personification Ideas or objects are written about as if they are human.		like a rusty iron gate
Simple sentence A sentence made up of a single clause; it has a subject and one main verb.		'There!' cried Sarah. 'The house is there.'
Verb A word that identifies actions or states of being.		clammy
Adjective A word that describes a noun.		a coil of iron hair
Adverb A word or words which are used to modify or tell us more about verbs (and adjectives and even whole sentences).		the soulless gaze of the windows
Dialogue The representation of speech in a work of fiction.		engulfed

ACTIVITY 3

In order to get a Grade 5, you will need to explain how the writer is using the technique in order to achieve a specific effect. Complete these two paragraphs by explaining why you think the writer has included the techniques.

a) *The writer varies sentences in her description of the house. For example, she writes in a short, simple sentence that 'It looked dead'. This helps to give the impression that*

....

....

b) *The writer then goes on to personify the house. The windows are described as having a 'soulless gaze' as they stare at the garden. This suggests* ....

....

....

Commenting on structure

In the exam, you may face a question like the one below. Notice that the second bullet point prompts you to consider the **structure** of the extract, as well as the language.

> How does the writer create a sense of fear and dread in these lines?
> You should write about:
> - what happens in these lines to create a sense of fear and dread
> - the writer's use of language and **structure** to create a sense of fear and dread
> - the effects on the reader.

To identify significant structural choices the writer has made in a text, you need to take a 'step back' from the extract. You need to track the sequence in which the writer achieves an effect.

This is not a checklist, but the following are useful features to consider:

- **significant changes in focus** – for example, the text may change from describing a setting to describing a character, or from describing a character's thoughts to dialogue

- **repetition** of ideas, images or significant words across the extract

- **contrasting** ideas, characters or settings

- **foreshadowing** – this is when a writer provides a hint about something which might happen later on.

EXAM TIP

When writing about how an author has structured the text, make sure you do not simply retell the events. Identify where there is a change in focus and explore the effects in relation to the question.

ACTIVITY 4

Answering the following questions will help you to consider how the writer of *The Silent Companions* extract on pages 14–15 has structured the extract to create a sense of fear and dread.

a) In the first paragraph, how does the writer foreshadow (hint) that the house is going to be unsettling and unpleasant?

....

....

b) The writer uses dialogue to indicate that the house has come into view: '"There!" cried Sarah.' How might this add to the sense of unease?

....

....

c) Look again at the paragraph beginning 'Everything was dead.' How does the writer repeat the idea of 'death' in this paragraph? How might this add to the sense of fear and dread?

....

....

d) Towards the end of the passage, the focus changes from the house to the staff, who are waiting outside the house to greet their new mistress. How does Elsie feel about this? What do you think Elsie's relationship with the staff will be like as the novel progresses?

....

....

Your answers to some of the questions above could then be worked up into a paragraph in which you explain the effects of the structure of the passage and link it to how the writer has created a sense of fear and dread.

This is an extract taken from a Grade 5 response to this question.

The student has included a clear point, linking structure to the focus of the question.

Accurate use of subject terminology.

The writer has structured the text to contribute to the developing sense of dread. At the beginning of the extract, the writer uses foreshadowing to hint that the house is going to be unsettling and unpleasant. Before they reach the house, nobody comes out to greet them at the gatehouse. This suggests that the house will not be very welcoming for Elsie and Sarah and establishes a sense of dread about what may happen next. Also, Elsie dislikes 'the sensation of her clammy sleeve moving against her arm'. Elsie already feels uncomfortable and this foreshadows her arrival at the menacing house and its associations with death.

The student has included a range of relevant details and quotations to support the point being made.

Concise explanation of the effects of the structure, showing how the foreshadowing indicates what happens later in the extract and how it creates a sense of fear and dread.

ACTIVITY 4

e) Write your own paragraph, using some of your answers to questions b), c) and/or d) and the example Grade 5 paragraph to help you.

....

....

....

....

....

....

....

ACTIVITY 5

This extract is from later on in the same novel, The Silent Companions. *Elsie is spending her first night in the house.*

Nobody came to close the door or remove the food. Despairing, Elsie placed her untouched dinner tray on the floor and dropped back against the pillows.

When she awoke, the room was as black as a weeping veil. The fire had expired, leaving the air chill. The taint of that damned soup still hung in the air, making her stomach writhe. How could the maid just
5   leave it there to fester and grow foul? She would have to speak with the housekeeper in the morning.

It was then that she heard it: a low rasp, like a saw against wood. She went rigid.

Had she really heard that? The senses could play tricks in the dark. But then it came again. *Hiss.*

She did not want to deal with another problem tonight. Surely if she kept wrapped up with her eyes shut, the noise would go away? *Hiss, hiss.* A rhythmic, abrasive sound. *Hiss hiss, hiss hiss.*

How has the writer structured the text to create fear and tension? Consider how the focus changes, repetition and foreshadowing. Use the sample Grade 5 paragraph in Activity 4 to help you.

....

....

....

....

....

....

....

....

Selecting relevant quotations and details from the text

To achieve a Grade 5, you need to support your explanation of how the writer has used structure and language with a range of quotations and details from the text.

When selecting a quotation, you should:

■ ensure the quotation is relevant to the focus of the question

■ ensure the quotation is no longer than it needs to be

■ ensure the quotation clearly backs up the point you are making

■ try, where possible, to embed your quotation into your own sentences: this will make your writing more fluent and more concise

■ ensure it is an interesting quotation which will enable you to explain the effects successfully

■ pick out particular words to explain in even more detail, where possible.

Now read the following text and complete Activity 6 on page 21.

The extract is taken from Small Island *by Andrea Levy. The novel is set in 1948 and describes the struggles of immigrants from Jamaica as they try to make a life for themselves in London. In this extract, the narrator, Hortense, has just arrived in London to join her husband, Gilbert. He is showing her where they will be living.*

'I hope you're not bringing anything into the house that will smell?' the Englishwoman interrupted.

The question erased the smile from my face. Turning to her I said, 'I have only brought what I –'

But Gilbert caught my elbow. 'Come, Hortense,' he said, as if the woman had not uttered a word. 'Come, let me show you around.'

5　I followed him up the first stairs and heard the woman call, 'What about the trunk, Gilbert? You can't leave it where it is.'

Gilbert looked over my shoulder to answer her, smiling: 'Don't worry, Queenie. Soon come, nah, man.'

I had to grab the banister to pull myself up stair after stair. There was hardly any light. Just one bulb so dull it was hard to tell whether it was giving out light or sucking it in. At every turn on the stairs there was another

10　set of steep steps, looking like an empty bookshelf in front of me. I longed for those ropes and pulleys of my earlier mind. I was groping like a blind man at times with nothing to light the way in front of me except the sound of Gilbert climbing ahead. 'Hortense, nearly there,' he called out, like Moses from the top of the mountain. I was palpitating by the time I reached the door where Gilbert stood grinning, saying: 'Here we are.'

'What a lot of stairs. Could you not find a place with fewer stairs?'

15　We went into the room. Gilbert rushed to pull a blanket over the unmade bed. Still warm I was sure. It was obvious to me he had just got out of it. I could smell gas. Gilbert waved his arms around as if showing me a lovely view. 'This is the room,' he said.

All I saw were dark brown walls. A broken chair that rested one uneven leg on the Holy Bible. A window with a torn curtain and Gilbert's suit – the double-breasted one – hanging from a rail on the wall.

20　'Well,' I said, 'show me the rest, then, Gilbert.' The man just stared. 'Show me the rest, nah. I am tired from the long journey.' He scratched his head. 'The other rooms, Gilbert. The ones you busy making so nice for me you forgot to come to the dock.'

Gilbert spoke so softly I could hardly hear. He said: 'But this is it.'

'I am sorry?' I said.

25　'This is it, Hortense. This is the room I am living.'

Three steps would take me to one side of this room. Four steps could take me to another. There was a sink in the corner, a rusty tap stuck out from the wall above it. There was a table with two chairs – one with its back broken – pushed up against the bed. The armchair held a shopping bag, a pyjama top, and a teapot. In the fireplace the gas hissed with a blue flame.

30 'Just this?' I had to sit on the bed. My legs gave way. There was no bounce underneath me as I fell. 'Just this? This is where you are living? Just this?'

'Yes, this is it.' He swung his arms around again, like it was a room in a palace.

'Just this? Just this? You bring me all this way just for this?'

The man sucked his teeth and flashed angry eyes in my face. 'What you expect woman? Yes, just this!
35 What you expect? Everyone live like this. There has been a war. Houses bombed. I know plenty of people live worse than this. What you want? You should stay with your mamma if you want it nice. There been a war here. Everyone live like this.'

He looked down at me, his badly buttoned chest heaving. The carpet was threadbare in a patch in the middle and there was a piece of bread lying on it. He sucked his teeth again and walked out the room. I
40 heard him banging down the stairs. He left me alone.

He left me alone to stare on just this.

ACTIVITY 6

Read lines 8–14.

How does the writer show you Hortense's feelings about her journey up the stairs in these lines?

You must refer to the language used in the text to support your answer, using relevant subject terminology where appropriate.   [5]

a) A student has highlighted three quotations in preparation for their response to this example exam question. Which two do you think are more likely to lead to a **successful response to this question** and why?

....

....

....

....

I had to grab the banister to pull myself up stair after stair. There was hardly any light. Just one bulb so dull it was hard to tell whether it was giving out light or sucking it in. At every turn on the stairs there was another set of steep steps, looking like an empty bookshelf in front of me. I longed for those ropes and pulleys of my earlier mind. I was groping like a blind man at times with nothing to light the way in front of me except the sound of Gilbert climbing ahead. 'Hortense, nearly there,' he called out, like Moses from the top of the mountain. I was palpitating by the time I reached the door where Gilbert stood grinning, saying: 'Here we are.'

'What a lot of stairs. Could you not find a place with fewer stairs?'

b) Circle two more relevant quotations from the extract above. Around the text, write a brief explanation of how they show you Hortense's feelings **about her journey up the stairs**.

EXAM TIP

Avoid making general comments and observations on your quotations that could apply to any passage. Instead, you should explain the effects of the quotations in relation to the specific text.

ACTIVITY 7

A student has written the following paragraph as part of a Grade 5 response to the exam question in Activity 6:

How does the writer show you Hortense's feelings about her journey up the stairs?

a) Annotate the paragraph where you have found evidence of the following:

- The quotation is not too long.
- The quotation is 'embedded' in the student's own sentence.
- The quotation enables the student to successfully explain the effects of language choices.
- The student has picked out particular words within the quotation to analyse in even more detail.

> The writer shows that Hortense feels that climbing the stairs is difficult because there is not enough light. There is only one bulb, and Hortense can't tell whether 'it was giving out light or sucking it in'. This suggests the extent of the darkness and that Hortense therefore doesn't know how much further she has to climb. This adds to her discomfort as she climbs 'stair after stair'. The verb 'sucking' personifies the bulb and implies that it is deliberately making efforts to make the stairs dark and difficult for Hortense.

b) Using the paragraph above as a model to help you, write your own paragraph using some or all of the quotations you circled in Activity 6.

....

....

....

....

....

....

....

....

Writing your response

ACTIVITY 8

> Read lines 15–31.
>
> What impressions do you get of the room in these lines?
>
> *You must refer to the text to support your answer using relevant subject terminology where appropriate.* [10]

A student has annotated the extract with some ideas in response to this question. They have started to explain the effects created by some of these language choices.

a) Complete the annotations in the space provided to explain how the specific examples add to your overall impressions of the room. The first two have been completed for you.

b) Now underline and annotate two further examples from the passage which add to your own impressions of the room.

> The writer uses colour. The adjectives 'dark' and 'brown' give the impressions that the room is dirty and there is a lack of light, like the stairs earlier in the extract.

We went into the room. Gilbert rushed to pull a blanket over the unmade bed. Still warm I was sure. It was obvious to me he had just got out of it. I could smell gas. Gilbert waved his arms around as if showing me a lovely view. 'This is the room,' he said.

All I saw were dark brown walls. A broken chair that rested one uneven leg on the Holy Bible. A window with a torn curtain and Gilbert's suit – the double-breasted one – hanging from a rail on the wall.

> The image here of Gilbert showing a 'lovely view' suggests how he wants to not disappoint Hortense. It contrasts with the reality of the room described in the rest of the passage.

'Well,' I said, 'show me the rest, then, Gilbert.' The man just stared. 'Show me the rest, nah. I am tired from the long journey.' He scratched his head. 'The other rooms, Gilbert. The ones you busy making so nice for me you forgot to come to the dock.'

Gilbert spoke so softly I could hardly hear. He said: 'But this is it.'

'I am sorry?' I said.

'This is it, Hortense. This is the room I am living.'

Three steps would take me to one side of this room. Four steps could take me to another. There was a sink in the corner, a rusty tap stuck out from the wall above it. There was a table with two chairs – one with its back broken – pushed up against the bed. The armchair held a shopping bag, a pyjama top, and a teapot. In the fireplace the gas hissed with a blue flame.

> The adjectives 'broken' and 'torn' suggest
> ....
> ....
> ....

'Just this?' I had to sit on the bed. My legs gave way. There was no bounce underneath me as I fell. 'Just this? This is where you are living? Just this?'

> Hortense's repetition of the question 'Just this?' suggests
> ....
> ....
> ....

> This rule of three gives the impression that
> ....
> ....
> ....

ACTIVITY 9

a) Read the paragraph below which is taken from a student's response to the question you considered in Activity 8. This response is likely to achieve a Grade 3. Think about how the paragraph could be improved by reading the teacher's comments and answering the questions on a separate piece of paper.

This is an accurate identification of a feature. However, how can you show an understanding that this feature is part of the writer's deliberate crafting of the text?

This explanation is too general. How can you make the explanation specific to the text itself? Can you connect the quotation to other things you learn about the room?

> Towards the end of the passage, there is a rule of three. 'The armchair held a shopping bag, a pyjama top, and a teapot. In the fireplace, the gas hissed.' These are ordinary, everyday items. They show how there isn't much space in the room and that the room is untidy.

This quotation does help to support your point but how can you shorten it and make it more precise?

This sentence shows a clear understanding. Why has the writer chosen these three particular objects, do you think?

b) Now read the student's improved version. If the rest of the answer reached this level of performance, it would be on course to achieve a Grade 5. Look at how the student has responded to the teacher's suggestions and improved the paragraph.

> Towards the end of the passage, the writer uses the rule of three as she lists the ordinary items Gilbert has left on the armchair. The chair holds a 'shopping bag, a pyjama top, and a teapot'. These objects give the impression that the room is untidy and that Gilbert does not have enough space to store even these three items. The objects, along with the room itself, give the impression that Gilbert might not have much money to support Hortense.

ACTIVITY 10

a) Read the paragraph below which is taken from another student's response to the question you considered in Activity 8. This response is likely to achieve a Grade 3. Complete the table beneath to identify how it could be improved.

> The writer says that the chairs are 'broken' and that there is a window with a curtain which is torn. These phrases show that the chairs are not working properly and that they have not been very well cared for or looked after. Gilbert does not seem to care about the room and he has lied to his wife about how good it is.

	Yes	No	Maybe
Does the student show an understanding that the writer has deliberately crafted the text?			
Does the student identify a technique and use subject terminology accurately?			
Has the student quoted clearly and concisely?			
Does the quotation support the point being made?			
Is there a clear explanation of the effects of the language used?			
Does the student make sure they answer the question by writing about their impressions of the room in the extract?			

b) Now write an improved version of the paragraph in the space provided. Use Activities 9 and 10 a) to help you.

c) Now write another paragraph in answer to the same question. Use your answers to the previous activities to help you.

EXAM TIP

Make sure your answers range across the whole extract. Do not, for example, make all your points on the first two or three sentences of the extract.

ACTIVITY (11)

The following relates to the extract from *Small Island* on pages 20–21.

> Read lines 32–41.
>
> How does the writer show the character of Gilbert in these lines?
>
> You should write about:
>
> ■ what Gilbert does and says in these lines
>
> ■ the writer's use of the language to show his character.
>
> *You must refer to the text to support your answer, using relevant subject terminology.* [10]

a) Underline the words and phrases you feel suggest something about the character of Gilbert and also identify any methods the writer is using.

b) Now write two paragraphs in response to the exam question. Make sure you:

■ include a clear point on how the writer is using language to show the character of Gilbert

■ include subject terminology

■ ensure your quotations are relevant and concise

■ focus in more detail on explaining the effects of a word in the quotation, where possible

■ provide detailed explanation of the effects

■ maintain a clear focus on the character of Gilbert.

Extended practice

Now that you have practised the skills in this chapter, it is time to write a complete response to Questions 2, 3 and 4 for Component 1.

After you have read the text below, give yourself 30 minutes in total to write your responses to the questions (up to seven minutes for Question 2, 10–12 minutes each for Questions 3 and 4).

Write your answers on a separate piece of paper.

Remember that to get a Grade 5 you will need to:

- develop a clear understanding of the text by reading it carefully all the way through before you answer the questions – consider what happens; what we learn about character/setting; what you think the writer is trying to achieve
- read the three questions carefully and underline key words and phrases in the question
- use subject terminology (but avoid feature-spotting)
- comment on structure where possible and appropriate (Question 4 below might offer some opportunities to consider structure)
- select relevant quotations and details from the text
- focus on the relevant passage specified in each question
- pick out key words from the quotation to explain effects in even more detail
- explain clearly the effects of language used and avoid general or vague comments.

The following extract is taken from Susan Hill's novel Strange Meeting. *The novel is partly set in the trenches of the First World War. In the extract, Barton is experiencing the realities of trench warfare for the first time. He is being guided along the trenches by a 'runner', a man called Grosse.*

When they began to make their way along the front line trench, Barton felt excitement churning in the pit of his stomach. It was his first real job, one for which he was entirely responsible, he had nobody, not even John, behind him. Only the runner, Grosse, guiding his way.

He had not been prepared for the full extent of the noise, which was deafening when the shells came
5 over. They were falling very close but they were mainly the heavy sort, which came with a sudden roar and at such speed that escape was impossible. You could do nothing about them, moreover, could not predict in advance where they might land, and so you simply went on, trusting to luck.

The trench was quite deep, cut into the chalk, and at the beginning the sandbags had been renewed and the **parapets** built up again. But as they went further on, work had ceased, the floor was a mess of
10 rubble, and the sides badly broken. Pit props, shovels and bales of wire cluttered every traverse, and the duckboards, laid in preparation for the coming winter, and the wet weather, were often broken or rotted away.

Grosse went ahead steadily, vanishing every few yards round a traverse, so that Barton felt he was following his own shadow, felt time and again he was completely alone. The chalk of the trench was
15 bright, dazzling his eyes in the midday sun. But he was exhilarated, glad that he had chosen to come here. There was an element of chance, but that did not yet seem to be the same thing as danger.

The shells were whining down often and seemed to be falling in a direct line ahead of them as they walked. Barton came around a traverse and almost bumped into his guide.

'What is it?'

20 Grosse had his head slightly on one side. 'Just seeing which way they're coming, sir. They're working them to a pattern.'

Parapets: a protective wall

There was a pause, and then, from nowhere, the loudest explosion Barton had ever heard, his eardrums seemed to crack and his head sang, the whole trench rocked as though from an earthquake. Just ahead, soil was thrown up like lava, and then there was the sound of it splattering down, mingled with
25 pieces of shrapnel, into the trench bottom. As they moved on a few paces, they heard a scream, which came with a curious, high, swooping sound and then dropped abruptly, became a moan. Then, behind them this time, another shell.

Grosse had thrown himself down, his hands over the top of his steel helmet, pushing it almost into his skull, but Barton had only dropped on his knees. His heart was thudding.

30 'Grosse?'

The man moved, lifted his head. 'Are you alright, sir?'

'Are *you*?'

The runner stood up cautiously, brushing down his tunic. His face was still impassive. He nodded.

'Shall we go on then?'

35 But as they rounded the next corner walking towards the spot from which the cry for stretcher bearers had just gone up, they came upon a total blockage in the trench-way, a mess of burst sandbags and earth, shrapnel and mutilated bodies. Blood had splattered up and over the parapet and was trickling down again, was running to form a pool, mingling with the contents of a **dixie** which had contained stew. The men had been getting their mid-day meal in this traverse when the bomb had landed in the middle
40 of them.

'Grosse …'

'Better hold on, sir.'

'Stretcher bearers!'

Barton said, 'Is there an officer here?'

35 A man was crouching, knees buckled and apparently broken beneath him, and he looked up now, his face white and the eyes huge with it. 'There was, sir.' He vomited, shuddered, wiped his mouth on his tunic sleeve.

Grosse leaned over him.

It was impossible to tell how many men there had been, and now the shells were landing again,
45 following the line of the trench further ahead. Barton wondered if they were going to meet a scene like this at every corner. He found himself staring in fascination at the shattered heap of limbs and helmets, at a bone sticking out somehow through the front of a tunic, at the blood. He felt numb.

The stretcher bearers came up, and sent back at once for more help, to dig the men out and clear up the mess. The trench parapet had a hole blown out of it like a crater.

50 'We could go on, sir,' Grosse said eventually. His voice was calm.

Dixie: a large cooking pot

Question 2

Read lines 1–16.

In these lines, how does the writer show you Barton's first experience of trench warfare?

You must refer to the language used in the text to support your answer, using relevant subject terminology.

[5]

Question 3

Read lines 17–27.

What impression do you get of the explosion in these lines?

You must refer to the text to support your answer, using relevant subject terminology.   [10]

Question 4

Read lines 28 to 50.

How does the writer show you the impact of the explosion?

You should write about:

■ what happens in these lines to show the impact of the explosion

■ the writer's use of language and structure to show the impact of the explosion

■ the effects on the reader.

You must refer to the text to support your answer, using relevant subject terminology.   [10]

CHECK YOUR PROGRESS

You have now practised the skills needed for Component 1, Questions 2, 3 and 4. Read through your answers to the Extended Practice questions. Use different coloured pens to highlight sections of your answers which show you have achieved the criteria in the table below.

Then tick the statements which apply to your answers.

	✔
I have a clear overall understanding of the extract.	
My responses are all relevant to the focus in the questions.	
I can use subject terminology accurately.	
I can select relevant quotations and details from the text.	
I can explain clearly the effects of language and structure and avoid vague or general observations.	
Where possible, I can pick out key words to explain the effects in more detail.	

Your reflections

Reflect on your answers and the progress check you completed. Which elements of these questions do you feel more confident about? Which areas do you feel you still need to work on?

....

....

....

....

....

Question 5: Critically evaluating a fiction text

For Question 5 you will need to show that you can evaluate how effective a fiction text is. This means you will need to develop a personal judgement about the extract and the choices made by the writer. You may be asked for your own opinion on an aspect of the text, such as character or setting, or you may need to say how far you agree with a given statement on the text.

The question is worth ten marks. You should aim to spend about 10–15 minutes answering the question.

Example exam question

This is reminding you of the importance of evaluation – be prepared to give your own view on the text.

Remember to focus primarily on the specific lines of the extract (although you will need to consider the passage as a whole as well).

Work out the key words in the question that tell you what to focus on. In this case, the key words are 'horror and disgust' towards the character.

The 'how' here is reminding you that you need to look at the language and structure of the text to support your view.

Read from line 12 to the end of the passage.

'In the last 17 lines, the writer makes you feel horror and disgust towards Ben.' How far do you agree with this view?

You should write about:

- your own thoughts and feelings about how Ben is presented here and in the passage as a whole
- how the writer has created these thoughts and feelings.

You must refer to the text to support your answer.

You are not required to agree entirely with the view expressed. Try to consider both sides of the argument if you can.

Remember to quote from the text.

How do I achieve a Grade 5 in my response to this question?

You will need to satisfy the following criteria in order to achieve a Grade 5 for Component 1, Question 5:

- Your evaluation – your own assessment of the text and its effects – needs to be clear.
- Your understanding of the text and some of the methods the writer uses needs to be secure.
- You need to select a range of relevant textual references and quotations.
- You need to ensure your response is relevant to the focus of the question/statement.

What does 'evaluate' mean?

When you evaluate a text, you are providing your own personal response and assessment of the text. When readers respond to texts, they do so in different ways. There is no 'fixed' interpretation. The examiner is looking for your own response which is well supported by quotations and textual details.

In the following extract, from Milly Jafta's short story, 'The Homecoming', a mother has returned to her home village and her daughter, Maria, after many years away.

Maria bent down and kissed me on the lips – a dry and unemotive gesture. She smiled, picked up the larger of the two suitcases and placed it on her head. Then she started walking ahead of me. I picked up the other case, placed it on my head and put both my hands in the small of my back to steady myself. Then I followed her. I looked at Maria's straight back, the proud way she held her head and the
5 determination with which she walked. I tried desperately to think of something to say, but could not find the words. Thoughts were spinning in my head, but my mouth remained closed and empty. So we continued in silence, this stranger – my daughter – and I.

ACTIVITY 1

Evaluate the way the writer presents the relationship between the mother and her daughter in this passage.

a) In preparing for a response to this question, Student A wrote the following:

I think that the relationship between the mother and the daughter is shown to be very cold and distant.

Find two quotations from the text to support this interpretation.

i ....

....

ii ....

....

b) In preparing for a response to this question, Student B wrote the following:

I think the writer is showing a connection and a hidden closeness in the relationship between the mother and the daughter.

Find two quotations from the text to support this interpretation.

i ....

....

ii ....

....

c) What is your view? Which interpretation do you think is the most convincing? Or do you have another interpretation of your own?

....

....

....

....

31

Reading the text and thinking about the question

This extract is taken from a novel by Doris Lessing called The Fifth Child. *The focus of the extract is on Harriet's 18-month-old child, Ben.*

When she went down again, the children were crowding around the dead dog. And then the adults came, and it was obvious what they thought.

Of course, it was impossible – a small child killing a lively dog. But officially the dog's death remained a mystery; the vet said it had been strangled. This business of the dog spoiled what was left of the
5 holidays, and people went off home early.

Dorothy said, 'People are going to think twice about coming again.'

Three months later, Mr McGregor, the old grey cat, was killed in the same way. He had always been afraid of Ben, and kept out of reach. But Ben must have stalked him, or found him sleeping.

At Christmas the house was half empty.

10 It was the worst year of Harriet's life, and she was not able to care that people avoided them. Every day was a long nightmare. She woke in the morning, unable to believe she would ever get through to the evening. Ben was always on his feet, and had to be watched every second. He slept very little. He spent most of the night standing on his window-sill, staring into the garden, and if Harriet looked in on him, he would turn and give her a long stare, alien, chilling: in the half dark of the room he really did look like a
15 little troll or a hobgoblin crouching there. If he was locked in during the day, he screamed and bellowed so that the whole house resounded with it, and they were all afraid the police would arrive. He would suddenly, for no reason she could see, take off and run into the garden, and then out the gate and into the street. One day, she ran a mile or more after him, seeing only that stubby squat little figure going through the traffic lights, ignoring cars that hooted and people who screamed warnings at him. She was
20 weeping, panting, half crazed, desperate to get to him before something terrible happened, but she was praying, Oh, do run him over, do, yes, *please* … She caught up with him just before a main road, grabbed him and held the fighting child with all her strength. He was spitting and hissing, while he jerked like a monster fish in her arms. A taxi went by; she called to it, she pushed the child in, and got in after him, holding him fast by an arm that seemed would break with his flailing about and fighting.

25 What could be done? Again she went to Dr Brett, who examined him and said he was physically in order.

Harriet described his behaviour and the doctor listened.

From time to time, a well-controlled incredulity appeared on his face, and he kept his eyes down, fiddling with pencils.

ACTIVITY 2

Here is the quotation again from the example question on page 30:

'From line 12, the writer makes you feel horror and disgust towards Ben.'

Focussing on line 12 to the end of the passage, highlight or underline quotations that make you feel horror and disgust towards Ben.

ACTIVITY 3

Look at the annotations that a student has made to prepare for a response to the exam question on page 30. The student has focussed on their own thoughts and feelings towards Ben and how these are created. Complete the empty boxes with annotations of your own.

> ....
> ....
> ....
> ....

> This is an unusual and unsettling action for a boy to be carrying out and makes me think of how Ben stalked the cat earlier in the passage.

> Adjectives suggesting how remote Ben is from his mother as well as his monstrous lack of humanity.

He spent most of the night standing on his window-sill, staring into the garden, and if Harriet looked in on him, he would turn and give her a long stare, alien, chilling: in the half dark of the room he really did look like a little troll or a hobgoblin crouching there. If he was locked in during the day, he screamed and bellowed so that the whole house resounded with it, and they were all afraid the police would arrive.

> Could this explain Ben's behaviour? His mother seems to imprison him. I feel a bit sorry for Ben here.

> ....
> ....
> ....
> ....

EXAM TIP

If you are given a statement to respond to in the exam, see if you can find any evidence which goes against or disagrees with the opinion expressed. Your response to a character, action or setting may also change as the text develops.

ACTIVITY 4

a) How do the following quotations make you feel towards Ben?

> she was praying, Oh, do run him over, do, yes, *please* …

This quotation makes me feel .... towards Ben because ....

....

> A taxi went by; she called to it, she pushed the child in, and got in after him, holding him fast by an arm that seemed would break …

This quotation makes me feel .... towards Ben because ....

....

b) Do you think Ben is as bad as his mother seems to think? Are her actions justified, do you think?

....
....
....
....

How to write a Grade 5 response to this question

In your answer to Component 1, Question 5 you need to ensure that you:

- show you have a secure overall understanding of the text as a whole
- consider your own personal response to the text and, where appropriate, consider the statement given in the question
- make detailed references to the text, including quotations
- explore and evaluate the writer's use of language and techniques.

Here is a reminder of the question you have been working on:

Read from line 12 to the end of the passage.

'In the last 17 line, the writer makes you feel horror and disgust towards Ben.' How far do you agree with this view?

You should write about:

- your own thoughts and feelings about how Ben is presented here and in the passage as a whole
- how the writer has created these thoughts and feelings.

You must refer to the text to support your answer.

ACTIVITY 5

a) Decide to what extent you agree that the writer 'makes you feel horror and disgust towards Ben'. Mark your personal judgement on the scale below with a cross.

Strongly disagree ——————————————————— Strongly agree

b) Summarise your view on the text in relation to the statement in one or two sentences.

....

....

....

....

ACTIVITY 6

a) Read paragraph A below. How could it be improved to a Grade 5 standard? Use the checklist to help you.

> **A** Ben is shown to be a horrific child in this passage. He stares into the garden whilst standing on a window-sill. 'He spent most of the night standing on his window-sill, staring into the garden.' Later on, he behaves like an animal when his mother tries to put him in a taxi and he struggles.

Has this student:
- shown they have a secure overall understanding of the text?
- considered in detail the statement given in the question?
- made quotations and provided detailed references to the text?
- explored and evaluated the writer's use of language and techniques?

b) Using the completed checklist above, write down a key piece of advice you would give this student in order to help them to achieve a Grade 5.

....

....

....

c) Read the Grade 5 paragraph B below to see how it is an improvement on paragraph A.

This is a clear and more detailed point than paragraph A.

Unlike paragraph A, this paragraph focuses on the writer's methods.

> **B** Throughout this passage, Ben is shown to be more of a horrific animal than a human. Ben, we learn, probably kills the dog and cat. Later, when his mother tries to put him in a taxi, he is 'spitting and hissing'. These verbs are commonly associated with animals and suggest Ben's difficult, repulsive behaviour. The writer also uses a simile when Ben is described as being 'like a monster fish' in his mother's arms, successfully implying both his strength and his disgusting, slippery movements. Ben is therefore presented more as a monster than a child, and this makes me feel disgust and unease about what he is capable of doing.

There are more detailed references to the text than Paragraph A, including a reference to the dog and cat from earlier in the passage. The quotations are concise and integrated into the sentences and there is a range of evidence to support the points being made.

Clear and concise explanation of the effects of the verbs.

This is a successful link to the statement in the question and provides a clear evaluation.

d) Read the Grade 5 paragraph C below. Annotate it with examples of the following:
- a secure overall understanding of the text
- consideration of the statement given in the question
- detailed references to the text, including quotations
- exploration and evaluation of the writer's use of language.

ACTIVITY 6

> **C** Ben is, however, more than a monstrous animal in this extract. I also feel sympathy for him because of the way his mother treats him. We learn that she locks him in his room during the day. Also, when he tries to escape, Harriet 'grabbed him' and 'pushed' him into a taxi. These strong, violent verbs suggest his mother does not love or care for him and makes me think that maybe Ben is behaving this way because of how she treats him. So although I agree that we are meant to feel 'horror and disgust' towards Ben, I also feel some pity towards him as well.

e) Using paragraphs B and C in the previous activities as models, write another paragraph in response to the same question. Use some of the annotations from previous activities to help you as well.

....

....

....

....

....

....

....

....

Extended practice

Read the text on page 37 and write a response to the example Component 1, Question 5 below. After reading the text, limit yourself to 15 minutes, which is how long you should spend answering this question in the exam.

Remember to consider and apply the skills covered in this chapter:

- Make sure you read the question and the text carefully.
- Remember to evaluate the text and develop your own personal response.
- Consider the effects of the language and structure of the passage in your response.
- Make sure you quote and provide detailed references to the text.

Evaluate the way the writer presents Hotense (the narrator) in this passage.

You should write about:

■ your thoughts and feelings about how Hortense is presented

■ how the writer creates these thoughts and feelings.

You must refer to the text to support your answer.

This extract is taken from Andrea Levy's novel, Small Island. *Hortense, the narrator, has just arrived in England from Jamaica. Mrs Bligh, her landlady, is taking her shopping.*

Now the man serving … had hair that was red. His face was speckled as a bird's egg with tiny red freckles. Scottish. I believed him to be Scottish. For in Jamaica it is only Scottish people that are red, but no, he too was English.

'What can I do you for?' he asked me directly. A red Englishman!

5 'He wants to know if you'd like anything,' Mrs Bligh told me.

I obliged her concern by making a purchase. 'A tin of condensed milk, please,' I asked him.

But this red man stared back at me as if I had not uttered the words. No light of comprehension sparkled in his eye. 'I beg your pardon?' he said.

Condensed milk, I said, five times, and he still looked on me bewildered. Why no one in this country
10 understand my English? At college my diction was admired by all. I had to point at the wretched tin of condensed milk, which resided just behind his head.

'Oh, condensed milk,' he told me, as if I had not been saying it all along.

Tired of this silly dance of miscomprehension, I did not bother to ask for the loaf of bread – I just point to the bread on the counter. The man enclose his big hand over the loaf, his freckled fingers spreading
15 across it. I stared on him. Was I to eat this bread now this man had touch it up? With his other hand he wiped his nose as he held out the bread for me to take. I did not take it, for I was waiting on him to place the bread into a bag to wrap it.

'There you are,' he said to me, pushing the loaf forward enough for me to see a think black line of dirt arching under each fingernail. It was Mrs Bligh who came and took the bread from him. Her dirty hand
20 having pinch my loaf as well, she placed it into my shopping bag.

Then she tell me loud for all to hear, 'This is bread.'

She think me a fool that does not know what is bread? But my mind could not believe what my eye had seen. That English people would buy their bread in this way. This man was patting on his red head and wiping his hand down his filthy white coat. Cha, why he no lick the bread first before giving it to me to eat?

25 I whispered in the ear of Mrs Bligh, 'He has not wrapped the bread.'

But she paid me no mind, so busy was she joining this shopkeeper in rolling their eyes to the heavens as I paid my money over.

CHECK YOUR PROGRESS

You have now practised the skills needed for a Grade 5 response to Component 1, Question 5. Read through your response to the Extended Practice task and use coloured highlighters to identify where you have satisfied the following criteria for Grade 5:

- clear personal evaluation of the text and its effects
- clear understanding of the text and some of the methods the writer uses
- selection of a range of relevant textual references and quotations
- the response is relevant to the focus of the question.

Your reflection

Reflect on your answers and the progress check you completed. Which elements of Component 1, Question 5 do you feel more confident about? Which areas do you feel you still need to work on?

....

....

....

....

....

Component 2, Section A: 19th and 21st Century Non-Fiction Reading

Questions 1 and 3: Identifying explicit and implicit information and ideas

For Component 2, Questions 1 and 3 you will be asked to identify information in the texts. The answers may be explicit or implicit. You will just need to find short quotations or summarise what is clearly there.

Question 1 will be on the first text (21st century). Question 3 will be on the second text (19th century). The questions will probably be broken down into smaller parts, such as a), b) and c).

There are three marks for each of these two questions. Aim to spend about three to five minutes on each question.

Example exam question

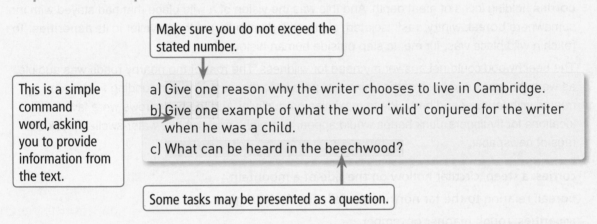

Make sure you do not exceed the stated number.

This is a simple command word, asking you to provide information from the text.

a) Give one reason why the writer chooses to live in Cambridge.

b) Give one example of what the word 'wild' conjured for the writer when he was a child.

c) What can be heard in the beechwood?

Some tasks may be presented as a question.

How do I achieve a Grade 5 in my response to these questions?

The aim of these questions is to allow you to get started and build confidence in dealing with each text. You should follow these four tips to help you to answer the questions and ensure you get as many marks as possible.

1 Make sure you are referring to the correct text and read each part of the question very carefully.

2 Do not waste time writing a lengthy answer or analysing the text.

3 Select the correct details from the text and write them down clearly.

4 Put your ideas into your own words or quote briefly from the text.

ACTIVITY ①

Read the four tips above on how to achieve a Grade 5 in your response to these questions. Make sure you follow the tips as you answer the three-part question below. The questions are on this extract from the non-fiction book *The Wild Places* by Robert Macfarlane:

Anyone who lives in a city will know the feeling of having been there too long. The gorge-vision that streets imprint on us, the sense of blockage, the longing for surfaces other than glass, brick, concrete and tarmac. I live in Cambridge, a city set in one of the most intensively farmed and densely populated regions of the world. It is an odd place for someone who loves mountains
5 and wildness to have settled. Cambridge is probably, hour for hour, about as far from what might conventionally be called 'wild land' as anywhere in Europe. I feel that distance keenly. But good things hold me there: my family, my work, my affection for the city itself, the way the stone of its old buildings condenses the light. I have lived in Cambridge on and off for a decade, and I imagine I will continue to do so for years to come. And for as long as I stay here, I know I will also have to get to
10 the wild places.

I could not now say when I first grew to love the wild, only that I did, and that a need for it will always remain strong in me. As a child, whenever I read the word, it conjured images of wide spaces, remote and figureless. Isolated islands off Atlantic coasts. Unbounded forests, and blue snow-light falling on to drifts marked with the paw-prints of wolves. Frost shattered summits and
15 **corries** holding lochs of great depth. And this was the vision of a wild place that had stayed with me: somewhere **boreal**, wintry, vast, isolated, elemental, demanding of the traveller in its **asperities**. To reach a wild place was, for me, to step outside human history.

The beechwood could not answer my need for wildness. The roar of the nearby roads was audible, as were the crash and honk of the trains that passed to the west. The surrounding fields were
20 treated with fertiliser and herbicide to maximise productivity. And the hedgerows were favourite locations for fly-tippers. Junk heaps would appear overnight: brick rubble, water-swollen plywood, rags of newspaper.

corries: a steep, circular hollow on the side of a mountain

boreal: relating to the far north, especially the Arctic region

asperities: rough manner or temper

a) Give one reason why the writer chooses to live in Cambridge.

....

....

b) Give one example of what the word 'wild' conjured for the writer when he was a child.

....

....

c) What can be heard in the beechwood?

....

....

ACTIVITY 2

Now check your responses to Activity 1 against these possible answers.

a) Any **one** from:

- his family
- his work/his job
- his affection for the city
- he likes the way the stone of its old buildings condenses the light.

b) Any **one** from:

- images of wide, remote spaces
- isolated islands off Atlantic coasts
- unbounded forests
- frosty mountains and deep corries.

c) The roar of nearby roads and the crash and honk of trains

Were any of your answers incorrect? If they were, check that you followed the four tips:

1 Make sure you are referring to the correct text and read each part of the question very carefully.

2 Do not waste time writing a lengthy answer or analysing the text.

3 Select the correct details from the text and write them down clearly.

4 Put your ideas into your own words or quote briefly from the text.

ACTIVITY 3

Read the extract below and the accompanying questions.

This extract is from History of a Six Weeks' Tour through a Part of France, Switzerland, Germany and Holland *by Mary Shelley and Percy Shelley.*

The mountains after St. Sulpice became loftier and more beautiful. We passed through a narrow valley between two ranges of mountains, clothed with forests, at the bottom of which flowed a river, from whose narrow bed on either side the boundaries of the vale arose **precipitously**. The road lay about half way up the mountain, which formed one of the sides, and we saw the overhanging rocks
5 above us and below, enormous pines, and the river, not to be perceived but from its reflection of the light of heaven, far beneath. The mountains of this beautiful ravine are so little asunder, that in time of war with France an iron chain is thrown across it. Two **leagues** from Neufchâtel we saw the Alps: range after range of black mountains are seen extending one before the other, and far behind all, towering above every feature of the scene, the snowy Alps. They were a hundred miles distant, but
10 reach so high in the heavens, that they look like those accumulated clouds of dazzling white that arrange themselves on the horizon during the summer. Their immensity staggers the imagination, and so far surpasses all conception, that it requires an effort of the understanding to believe they indeed form a part of the earth.

From this point we descended to Neufchâtel, which is situated in a narrow plain, between the
15 mountains and its immense lake, and presents no additional aspect of peculiar interest.

precipitously: very steep

leagues: an old measure of distance (usually about three miles)

ACTIVITY ③

A student has attempted to answer the following questions. Unfortunately, there is an error in each answer. In the space provided, explain the error you think the student has made. Then go on to write the correct answer.

a) How did the mountains change after St. Sulpice?

They were lofty and steep.

This answer is incorrect because ....

....

b) What is at the bottom of the narrow valley?

Forests

This answer is incorrect because ....

....

c) What is described as 'towering above every feature of the scene'?

The range of black mountains

This answer is incorrect because ....

....

ACTIVITY ④

This extract is taken from a guidebook to London called Walks in and around London, *written in 1895 by 'Uncle Jonathan'. It describes the children working in London's streets.*

If we went to Covent Garden Market at about five or six o'clock one morning, we should find many of these boys and girls waiting to purchase their stock in trade. There are the flower-girls, choosing and buying their bunches of flowers and fern-leaves, which they will carry to their homes. Arranging them there, and making them into neat little 'button-holes', they will sally forth after their meagre
5 meal, to the various railway stations from which the streams of City people are pouring into the streets. The sweet scent of their daintily arranged flowers, and their cry of 'Sweet Violets' soon bring customers. For busy City people like a flower, to remind them of what is beautiful outside the smoky town. Another early bird is the water-cress girl. She goes to market for the fresh young water-cress that is brought from the country in the early hours of the morning. Tying them into bunches as she
10 goes along, her cries of 'Water-cree-sue' will sometimes let us know it is time we, too, were up.

Read the above extract from the guidebook. Use the questions in Activities 1 and 2 as models, write a minimum of three questions on the extract. Make sure the questions only require short answers and that they ask to identify information from the text. You could then ask a student in your class or a friend to answer your own questions.

■ **Example question:** Where do the flower-girls sell their flowers?

■ **Question a):** ....

■ **Question b):** ....

■ **Question c):** ....

Extended practice

Answer the example Component 2, Question 3 below. After you have read the extract, limit yourself to five minutes, which is how long you should spend answering this question in the exam. Remember to consider and apply the skills and approaches covered in this chapter.

This extract is taken from an article in Household Words *(1857) by Charles Dickens. The extract describes the life of 'hovellers', who crew lifeboats on the coast of Kent.*

It is a dark night in December, and it blows a gale of wind. The hovelling world of **Broadstairs** is on the alert, for somebody has heard a gun, and it is expected that a ship is on shore in the **Godwin Sands**.

Some five-and-twenty men, all **hovellers**, are now congregated on the pier. Both lifeboats are in readiness, and so are the three **luggers**. How impatiently some of the men walk to and fro! That tall
5 and strongly-built man with the handsome features and open countenance is old Jem Taylor. If asked to guess his age, you would say five-and-forty; but to my knowledge he is over sixty-six. He served his thirty years in the Royal Navy, and was a **quartermaster** for twenty-two years of the period. He is now an out-pensioner of Greenwich Hospital, and draws his twenty-nine pounds per annum. There is scarcely a port in the world that he has not visited – East and West Indies, China, South America, Africa,
10 Australia. He has served in fourteen of Her Majesty's ships, and from every captain has a certificate that his conduct was very good, and that he was always obedient to command. Taylor has seen some hard fighting in his day, and wears upon his Sunday jacket several silver medals; but the medal of which he seems the most proud is the one awarded him for saving life.

If you ask why, at his time of life, and now that he is provided for by his pension, he engages in the
15 dangerous business of hovelling, he will tell you that he feels a young man still; that he likes the life of adventure, and that idleness would drive him mad.

Broadstairs: a coastal town in Kent

Godwin Sands: a sandbank (a bank of sand just below the surface of the sea) off the coast in Kent; in this extract, they fear a ship has been wrecked on the sandbank

hovellers: boatmen on the coast of Kent

luggers: a small sailing ship

quartermaster: the person who steers a ship in the Royal Navy

a) Give **one** detail of Jem Taylor's appearance.

....

b) When he served in the Royal Navy, what did Jem Taylor's captains think of his conduct?

....

c) Why does Jem Taylor still sail lifeboats?

....

CHECK YOUR PROGRESS

You have now practised the skills needed for a Grade 5 response to Component 1, Question 5. Read through your response and identify where you have satisfied the following criteria for Grade 5.

You have now practised the skills needed for Component 2, Questions 1 and 3. Read through your answers to the Extended Practice activity and check them against the possible answers below.

a) He is tall OR
   He is strongly-built OR
   He is handsome OR
   He has an open countenance OR
   He looks younger than he is.

b) His conduct was very good OR
   He always obeyed commands.

c) He still feels young and likes the adventure OR
   He likes to keep busy.

Your reflection

Reflect on your answers and the progress check you completed. How confident do you feel in answering these questions?

....

....

....

Question 2: Writing about language and structure

For Component 2, Question 2 you will be asked how the writer uses language and structure to convey a certain point of view or idea. The question will be on the first text, which will be a 21st century non-fiction text.

The question is worth ten marks. You should aim to spend about 10–12 minutes answering the question.

Example exam question

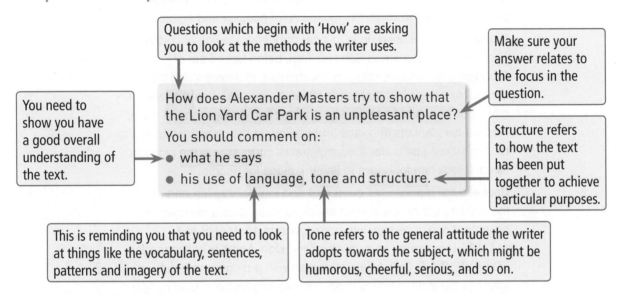

Questions which begin with 'How' are asking you to look at the methods the writer uses.

Make sure your answer relates to the focus in the question.

You need to show you have a good overall understanding of the text.

How does Alexander Masters try to show that the Lion Yard Car Park is an unpleasant place?
You should comment on:
● what he says
● his use of language, tone and structure.

Structure refers to how the text has been put together to achieve particular purposes.

This is reminding you that you need to look at things like the vocabulary, sentences, patterns and imagery of the text.

Tone refers to the general attitude the writer adopts towards the subject, which might be humorous, cheerful, serious, and so on.

How do I achieve a Grade 5 in my response to this question?

You will need to satisfy the following criteria in order to achieve a Grade 5 for Component 2, Question 2:

- Have a clear understanding of the text.
- Explain clearly the effects of language and structure.
- Select a range of relevant quotations and details from the text.
- Use subject terminology appropriately and accurately.

Selecting relevant quotations and details from the text

To achieve a Grade 5, you need to support your explanation of how the writer has used structure and language with a range of quotations and details from the text.

When selecting a quotation, you should:

- ensure the quotation is relevant to the focus of the question
- ensure the quotation is no longer than it needs to be
- ensure the quotation clearly backs up the point you are making
- try, where possible, to embed your quotation into your own sentences: this will make your writing more fluent and more concise
- ensure it is an interesting quotation which will enable you to explain the effects successfully
- pick out particular words to explain in even more detail, where possible.

ACTIVITY 1

This extract is taken from Stuart: A Life Backwards, by Alexander Masters. It is a biography of Stuart Shorter, a homeless man.

Lion Yard Car Park is a boat of a place. Its cargo hold, nine concrete storeys of smog and tyre burns, is topped by the glass-covered, centrally heated magistrates' court – the galley, so to speak. The prow of the boat – an eighth of a mile further south, under the Holiday Inn – thrusts towards the university museums of geology and anthropology.

Stuart aged 29 fetched up in this car park after leaving his mother's pub, meeting Asterix and Scouser Tom, being kicked out of Smudger's flat and messing up his chances at Jimmy's and the day centre. He'd been told that ten to fifteen people 'skippered' there every night, but wherever he looked he couldn't find a single one of them. He took his blankets and rags and walked up the circular staircase to the top storey, just under the magistrates' court, where the pigeons sleep. It took him four days to find the place for people.

Between the magistrates' court end and the Holiday Inn end of the building are ramps and an aerial walkway, plus a mezzanine basement dug, it seems, into pure concrete. HUMANS NOT ALLOWED indicates an accompanying sign. Another notice reads TO LEVELS A-B-C-D. A little stick man with a ping-pong head marches behind the letters in an encouraging manner, guiding you along a narrow pavement. Grey drops of chewing gum splatter the way, congesting towards a stair door and lift at the other end. Then Ping-Pong Head pops up again, on a sign hurrying back towards TOILETS. The pillars supporting the ceiling here (we are now under the Holiday Inn) are stencilled with the letter A. IS THIS [A]RT MUMMY? someone has scrawled around one …

On the other side of the door is the concrete staircase: cinder grey, regular. The banister is red. The smell is dust and disinfectant. Go down two flights. The walls still show the grain of the plywood moulds that once held them when they were poured. If you peer hard through the dark Perspex window in the door of this floor – Level B – you can often spot something interesting. Couples kissing passionately in the front seats, couples in the back seats, couples shouting. Depth, in this building, quickly gives a conviction of privacy. Down two more flights and Level C begins to show the strain. The walls are laterally cracked, like an exposed vein of a leaf. Occasionally, the smell loses its warm chemical hint and a waft of urine insinuates itself instead. There are still currents of air …

Above you, the noises could be of people leaving the staircase at the top; or, equally, stomping across the floor directly above. Sound is impossible to place.

Push through this door, out of the stairwell into Level D, and you will see in front of you 15,000 square feet of car park that is completely empty.

This is where the homeless sleep.

ACTIVITY 1

How does Alexander Masters try to show that the Lion Yard Car Park is an unpleasant place?
You should comment on:
- what he says
- his use of language, tone and structure.

[10]

a) A student has highlighted four quotations in preparation for their response to this example exam question. Which **two** do you think are more likely to lead to a successful response to this question on how the writers shows the car park to be an unpleasant place? Why?

....

....

....

....

b) Circle at least three more relevant quotations. Around the text, write a brief explanation of how they show you that the Lion Yard Car Park is an unpleasant place.

ACTIVITY 2

A student has written the following paragraph as part of a Grade 5 response to the exam question in Activity 1.

How does Alexander Masters try to show that the Lion Yard Car Park is an unpleasant place?

a) Annotate the paragraph where you have found evidence of the following:
- The quotations are not too long.
- The quotations are 'embedded' in the student's own sentence.
- The quotations enable the student to successfully explain the effects of language choices.
- The student has picked out particular words within a quotation to analyse in even more detail.

Alexander Masters' description of the chewing gum adds to the unpleasantness of the car park. He describes the 'grey drops of chewing gum' which 'splatter the way'. The adjective 'grey' adds to the dark, colourless qualities of the car park. The verb 'splatter' reminds the reader that the chewing gum has been left carelessly by many people and gives the impression that the car park is not very well looked after and is dirty and untidy. This lack of cleanliness is reinforced when Masters goes on to say that the pieces of gum are 'congesting toward the stair door'. The verb 'congesting' is similar to 'splatter' and suggests that there is an unhealthy amount of chewing gum.

ACTIVITY 2

b) Write your own paragraph in response to the same question. Use the paragraph above as a model to help you and remember to explain how it makes the car park an unpleasant place. Use at least one of the quotations you circled in Activity 1 b).

....

....

....

....

....

....

....

....

Using subject terminology

In order to get a Grade 5 for this question, you need to use subject terminology accurately. Some of the subject terminology you might use in Component 1 – such as metaphor and verb – will also be appropriate for this question.

The activities in this section will remind you of some of the subject terminology you are more likely to use when studying non-fiction texts for Component 2.

ACTIVITY 3

a) Listed in the table below are some methods a non-fiction writer might use to make their writing more engaging or persuasive. Match the term on the left with the definition on the right. The first has been completed for you.

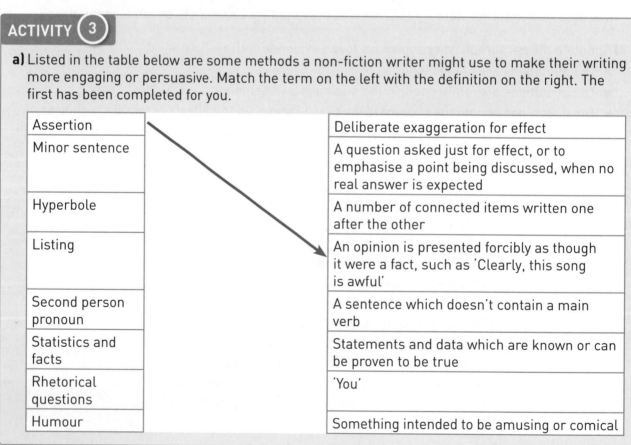

Term	Definition
Assertion	Deliberate exaggeration for effect
Minor sentence	A question asked just for effect, or to emphasise a point being discussed, when no real answer is expected
Hyperbole	A number of connected items written one after the other
Listing	An opinion is presented forcibly as though it were a fact, such as 'Clearly, this song is awful'
Second person pronoun	A sentence which doesn't contain a main verb
Statistics and facts	Statements and data which are known or can be proven to be true
Rhetorical questions	'You'
Humour	Something intended to be amusing or comical

ACTIVITY ③

b) Read the article by Rich Pelley from the *Guardian* below on Peppa Pig.

Peppa Pig: how the ham-fisted cartoon butchered its charm

While not without its controversies, the porcine kids' show matured into a true worldwide phenomenon. Then, like Skynet, it became too self-aware.

Kids are morons. You can't talk to them about Brexit, or Trump, or the theory of everything. No. You
5 have to tackle such philosophical questions as 'Why do I have to go to bed?' or 'Why do I have to have a bath?' Kids' TV-viewing habits are equally moronic. Take Peppa Pig, a British cartoon about four-year-old Peppa Pig and her family. There's younger brother George, Mummy Pig, Granny Pig, Grandpa Pig and Daddy Pig. Peppa's classmates are cats, dogs, sheep, zebras, elephants and ponies. Her teacher is a gazelle. It's the greatest multicultural school of all time.

10 At five minutes an episode, there is little room for cliffhangers or plot twists. In Windy Castle, the Pigs get lost on the way to Windy Castle, because Daddy Pig is navigating and Daddy Pig is rubbish at navigating. In Daddy Pig Puts Up a Picture, Daddy Pig knocks a giant hole in the wall, because Daddy Pig is rubbish at DIY. Each episode ends with everybody literally rolling around on the floor with laughter. Black Mirror, this is not.

15 Of course, you want to hate the banality of it. You want to punch Daddy Pig in the glasses for being so stereotypical. But you cannot help but get drawn in. Especially when you realise that kids are absolutely mesmerised by this piggy guff. To them, it's bacon heroin. Peppa Pig first aired for 208 episodes between 2004 and 2012, becoming a worldwide smash. Merchandise sales amounted to £200m in 2010 in the UK alone, and Peppa Pig World opened in Hampshire in 2011.

20 There has been controversy. The One Where Peppa and George Make Friends With Mr Skinny Legs the Spider is no longer shown in Australia. Dr Brown Bear's efficiency at jumping in his ambulance to prescribe antibiotics to anyone with as little as a cough was genuinely claimed by a GP to promote 'unrealistic expectations of primary care' in 2017. In 2018, Peppa Pig got into trouble in China after being adopted as a subversive gangster icon. Yes, really.

25 Peppa Pig was re-commissioned in 2016 (with guest voices from David Mitchell and Jo Brand) which, for any parent who had sat through every single episode a million times, came as a blessed relief. But, there was a problem. Like Skynet, Peppa Pig had become self-aware. There were subtle in-jokes aimed directly at the parents. No one's mummy or daddy wants to stay at Richard Rabbit's birthday party in Soft Play, for fear of getting stuck (SPOILER ALERT! Daddy
30 Pig gets stuck). Zoo Keeper Lion has to restrain himself from eating Madame Gazelle for lunch in The Zoo. Daddy Pig's car is a robot-dragon's footstep away from getting crushed when he ignores the parking warnings in The Castle. And the slapstick is turned up to 'adult' when Daddy Pig sets himself in concrete, Granny pig falls into a pile of manure, and Daddy Pig falls out of a plane with no parachute, Homer-Simpson-falling-down Springfield-Gorge-style.

35 Now, suddenly, the joke is on you. *You* are the idiot for getting sucked in. Peppa Pig's creators are multi-millionaires. What have you done with your life? You've been upstaged by a two dimensional pig, that's what. And you are simply too pig-headed to notice. Oink oink.

Skynet: a reference to the fictional intelligent computer network which appears in the *Terminator* films

Black Mirror: a television drama series associated with dark, serious issues

Homer-Simpson-falling-down Springfield-Gorge-style: a reference to a scene in the television cartoon series *The Simpsons* in which Homer Simpson falls a long way down a cliff

ACTIVITY ③

Find an example of each of the methods in Activity 3 a). The first has been completed for you.

Assertion: *You've been upstaged by a two dimensional pig, that's what.*

Minor sentence: ....

....

Hyperbole: ....

....

Listing: ....

....

Second person pronoun: ....

....

Statistics and facts: ....

....

Rhetorical questions: ....

....

Humour: ....

....

c) Now read this question, based on the same article from the *Guardian*.

> How does the writer, Rich Pelley, show you his opinions on Peppa Pig?

Which **two** quotations/methods from Activity 3 b) would you select in a response to this question and why?

....

....

....

....

....

ACTIVITY 3

d) Read this paragraph from a Grade 5 response to the same question. The accompanying annotations show how the student meets the criteria for a Grade 5 response.

A clear point on the writer's use of language. The student is clearly addressing the focus in the question.

A clear understanding of the writer's opinions on Peppa Pig.

Rich Pelley develops a humorous tone to show his opinions on Peppa Pig. He argues that the adults who enjoy watching Peppa Pig have been 'sucked in' by the show's intelligence. To help create this humour, he uses a rhetorical question, as he asks the reader 'What have you done with your life?' This suggests that the reader should feel ashamed and should feel that they have wasted their time watching the show.

Accurate use of subject terminology.

Relevant quotation.

Clear explanation of the effects of the quotation in relation to the question.

e) Using one of the quotations and methods you selected for Activity 3 c), write your own paragraph in the space provided below. Use the previous paragraph as a model to help you. Make sure you use subject terminology in your response.

....

....

....

....

....

....

....

....

....

EXAM TIP

Avoid 'feature spotting' in the exam. Only use subject terminology where it is appropriate to do so and when you can explain the effects of the technique.

Commenting on tone and structure

Component 2, Question 2 may also ask you to consider how the writer uses tone and/or structure, as well as language.

Tone refers to the general attitude the writer adopts towards the subject, which might be humorous, cheerful, serious, and so on.

Structure refers to how the text has been put together, such as how it engages the reader at the beginning, or how the writer concludes an argument at the end.

ACTIVITY (4)

Read the three extracts. Which word(s) do you think best describe the tone of each extract? You may choose more than one word for each extract. Go on to provide at least one quotation from the text which helps to create the tone.

Dark

Humorous

Cheerful

Official

Analytical

Depressing

Excited

Sympathetic

Thoughtful

Angry

Extract A: *The Wild Places* by Robert MacFarlane

I could not now say when I first grew to love the wild, only that I did, and that a need for it will always remain strong in me. As a child, whenever I read the word, it conjured images of wide spaces, remote and figureless. Isolated islands off Atlantic coasts. Unbounded forests, and blue snow-light falling on to drifts marked with the paw-prints of wolves. Frost shattered summits and **corries** holding lochs
5 of great depth. And this was the vision of a wild place that had stayed with me: somewhere **boreal**, wintry, vast, isolated, elemental, demanding of the traveller in its **asperities**. To reach a wild place was, for me, to step outside human history.

corries: a steep, circular hollow on the side of a mountain

boreal: relating to the far north, especially the Arctic region

asperities: rough manner or temper

The following word or words best describe the tone of this extract:

....

The following quotations help to create this tone:

....

....

Extract B: *Stuart: A Life Backwards* by Alexander Masters

Between the magistrates' court end and the Holiday Inn end of the building are ramps and an aerial walkway, plus a mezzanine basement dug, it seems, into pure concrete. HUMANS NOT ALLOWED indicates an accompanying sign. Another notice reads TO LEVELS A-B-C-D. A little stick man with a ping-pong head marches behind the letters in an encouraging manner, guiding you along a narrow
5 pavement. Grey drops of chewing gum splatter the way, congesting towards a stair door and lift at the other end. Then Ping-Pong Head pops up again, on a sign hurrying back towards TOILETS. The pillars supporting the ceiling here (we are now under the Holiday Inn) are stencilled with the letter A. IS THIS [A]RT MUMMY? someone has scrawled around one …

The following word or words best describe the tone of this extract:

....

ACTIVITY 4

The following quotations help to create this tone:

....

....

Extract C: *Guardian* article 'Peppa Pig: how the ham-fisted cartoon butchered its charm' by Rich Pelley

> Now, suddenly, the joke is on you. *You* are the idiot for getting sucked in. Peppa Pig's creators are multi-millionaires. What have you done with your life? You've been upstaged by a two dimensional pig, that's what. And you are simply too pig-headed to notice. Oink oink.

The following word or words best describe the tone of this extract:

....

The following quotations help to create this tone:

....

....

ACTIVITY 5

Read the extract from *Stuart: A Life Backwards* on page 46 then answer these questions on how the writer has structured the text.

a) How does the writer set the scene in the opening paragraph?

....

....

b) Why does the writer change the focus to Stuart in the second paragraph? How does he connect Stuart – the subject of the biography – to the Lion Yard Car Park?

....

....

c) How does the writer use the different levels of the car park to help him to structure the text? How does it help to make the car par unpleasant?

....

....

d) Why does the writer choose to end the extract with the single sentence paragraph 'This is where the homeless sleep'?

....

....

ACTIVITY 6

Read the following paragraph from a student's response to this question:

> How does Alexander Masters try to show that the Lion Yard Car Park is an unpleasant place?
>
> You should comment on:
> - what he says
> - his use of language, tone and structure.

In this paragraph, the student is explaining how the structure of the text helps Alexander Masters to show that the Lion Yard Car Park is an unpleasant place. Complete the paragraph, using your answer to Activity 5 c) to help you.

> The way Alexander Masters has structured the text helps convey the car park as an unpleasant place. It is as though he takes us on a tour. We begin in Level A, where he describes the graffiti. He then moves on to Level B, Level C (which starts to 'show the strain'), before opening the door to Level D: the lowest level where the homeless sleep. This structure helps to make the car park unpleasant because
>
> ....
>
> ....
>
> ....
>
> ....

Extended practice

Answer this example Component 2, Question 2. After you have read the extract, limit yourself to 12 minutes, which is how long you should spend answering the question in the exam. Remember to consider and apply the skills and approaches covered in this chapter.

The following is an article from the Independent *by Janet Street-Porter.*

> **Halloween is nothing more than legitimised begging by aggressive kids in costumes – I can't stand it**
>
> Very few things in this life make me anxious or fearful, but next Wednesday is already giving me plenty
> 5 of concern.
>
> Halloween has become an event feared and loathed by a silent majority who regard it as nothing more than legitimised begging by aggressive kids in silly costumes egged on by pushy mothers. This is a public announcement to all trick-or-treaters in my neighbourhood: I will not be at home, so don't bother turning up and ringing my doorbell like you did last year, on and off for three long hours. My letterbox will
> 10 be taped up so you can't scream through it.
>
> Where's the fun in all of this for older people and pets? By 4.30pm on Wednesday 31 October, it will be dark and excited packs of trick-or-treaters will be roaming the streets of our towns and cities looking for victims, acting out a low-budget horror movie in their heads.
>
> Later that evening, 'celebrities' will be forcing themselves into ludicrous costumes and silly wigs to be
> 15 photographed by the paparazzi in North London arriving at Jonathan Ross's Halloween party, just like they do every single year. Surely there's an easier way to get your picture in the press?

Fancy dress is another trial for me (not that I'm invited chez Ross). It's a chance to look your worst and feel a fool while paying a hire company for the privilege.

Halloween celebrations have got out of hand, so take my advice – disconnect the doorbell, get under
20 the duvet with a torch and a good book or your laptop, and turn off the lights. For a few short hours, you'll be under siege. Then it's over, for another year.

How does Janet Street-Porter try to persuade the reader that Halloween is to be 'feared and loathed'?

You should comment on:

■ what she says
■ her use of language and tone.   [10]

CHECK YOUR PROGRESS

You have now practised the skills needed for Component 2, Question 2. Read through your answers to the Extended Practice questions. Use different coloured pens to highlight sections of your answers which show you have achieved the criteria in the table below.

Then tick the statements which apply to your answers.

	✔
I have a clear overall understanding of the extract.	
My response is relevant to the focus in the question.	
I can use subject terminology accurately.	
I can select relevant quotations and details from the text.	
I can explain clearly the effects of language and avoid vague or general observations.	
I can explain clearly the effects of structure and/or tone.	
Where possible, I can pick out key words to explain the effects in more detail.	

Your reflections

Reflect on your answers and the progress check you completed. Which elements of these questions do you feel more confident about? Which areas do you feel you still need to work on?

....

....

....

....

....

Question 4: Critically evaluating a non-fiction text

For Question 4 you will need to show that you can evaluate how effective a fiction text is. This means you will need to develop a personal judgement about the extract and the choices made by the writer. The question will ask you what you feel or think about an aspect of the extract or how successful the writer is in conveying their ideas or achieving their purposes. You may need to say how far you agree with a given statement on the text.

Question 4 is worth ten marks. You should aim to spend about 10–12 minutes answering the question.

Example exam questions

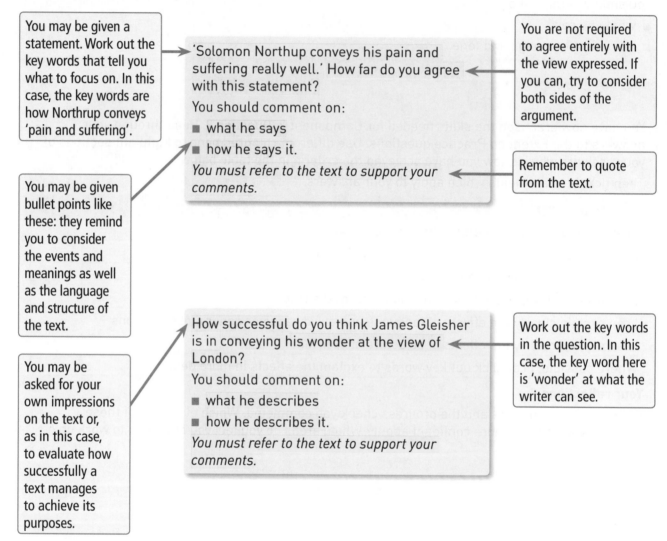

You may be given a statement. Work out the key words that tell you what to focus on. In this case, the key words are how Northrup conveys 'pain and suffering'.

You may be given bullet points like these: they remind you to consider the events and meanings as well as the language and structure of the text.

You may be asked for your own impressions on the text or, as in this case, to evaluate how successfully a text manages to achieve its purposes.

'Solomon Northup conveys his pain and suffering really well.' How far do you agree with this statement?
You should comment on:
■ what he says
■ how he says it.
You must refer to the text to support your comments.

You are not required to agree entirely with the view expressed. If you can, try to consider both sides of the argument.

Remember to quote from the text.

How successful do you think James Gleisher is in conveying his wonder at the view of London?
You should comment on:
■ what he describes
■ how he describes it.
You must refer to the text to support your comments.

Work out the key words in the question. In this case, the key word here is 'wonder' at what the writer can see.

How do I achieve a Grade 5 in my response to this question?

You will need to satisfy the following criteria in order to achieve a Grade 5 for Component 2, Question 4:
■ Your evaluation – your own assessment of the text and its effects – needs to be clear.
■ Your understanding of the text and some of the methods the writer uses needs to be secure.
■ You need to select a range of relevant textual references and quotations.
■ You need to ensure your response is relevant to the focus of the question.

There are further activities on developing your understanding of what is meant by evaluating a text in the chapter starting on page 30.

Reading the text and thinking about the question

Before you start writing your response to Question 4, you need to read the question and the text again. Think about your own personal response to the focus of the question. As you read the text, select some quotations and textual details to support your view.

ACTIVITY 1

Read the question and then go on to read the extract below from *Twelve Years a Slave*. Highlight or underline quotations that you feel convey the **pain** and **suffering** Northrup is experiencing. Annotate with a brief explanation of how your selected quotations convey Northup's pain and suffering.

'Solomon Northup conveys his pain and suffering really well.' How far do you agree with this statement?

You should comment on:

■ what he says
■ how he says it.

You must refer to the text to support your comments.   [10]

This extract is taken from Twelve Years a Slave *by Solomon Northup, first published in 1853. The book is an account of Northup's experiences as a slave in America. In this extract, having narrowly escaped being hanged by Tibeats, Northup is bound in rope in the hot sun.*

As the sun approached the **meridian** that day it became insufferably warm. Its hot rays scorched the ground. The earth almost blistered the foot that stood upon it. I was without coat or hat, standing bare-headed, exposed to its burning blaze. Great drops of perspiration rolled down my face, drenching the scanty apparel wherewith I was clothed. Over the fence, a very little way off, the peach trees cast their cool, delicious shadows on the grass. I would gladly have given a long year of service to have been enabled to exchange the heated oven, as it were, wherein I stood, for a seat beneath their branches. But I was yet bound, the rope still dangling from my neck, and standing in the same tracks where Tibeats and his comrades left me. I could not move an inch, so firmly had I been bound. To have been enabled to lean against the weaving-house would have been a luxury indeed. But it was far beyond my reach, though distant less than twenty feet. I wanted to lie down, but knew I could not rise again. The ground was so parched and boiling hot I was aware it would but add to the discomfort of my situation. If I could only have moved my position, however slightly, it would have been a relief unspeakable. But the hot rays of the southern sun, beating all the long summer day on my bare head, produced not half the suffering I experienced from my aching limbs. My wrists and ankles, and the cords of my legs and arms began to swell, burying the rope that bound them into the swollen flesh …

ACTIVITY 1

From long before daylight I had not eaten a morsel. I was growing faint from pain, and thirst, and hunger. Once only, in the very hottest portion of the day, Rachel, half fearful she was acting contrary to the overseer's wishes, ventured to me, and held a cup of water to my lips. The humble creature never knew, nor could she comprehend if she heard the blessings I invoked upon her, for that balmy draught. She could only say, 'Oh, Platt, how I do pity you,' and then hastened back to her labors in the kitchen.

Never did the sun move so slowly through the heavens – never did it shine down such fervent and fiery rays, as it did that day. At least, so it appeared to me. What my meditations were – the innumerable thoughts that thronged through my distracted brain – I will not attempt to give expression to. Suffice it to say, during the whole long day I came not to the conclusion, even once, that the southern slave, fed, clothed, whipped and protected by his master, is happier than the free colored citizen of the North. To that conclusion I have never since arrived.

meridian: noon

ACTIVITY 2

A student has highlighted and annotated a section of the same extract. Read through the annotations. Compare the student's annotations with your own. Are any quotations and annotations different from your own? Are any the same?

> The writer focuses my attention on the intense heat and how uncomfortable it is for him; 'burning' suggests extreme physical pain.

> Contrast with the 'delicious' shadows; I feel as though he is being tormented by the cool shade as it is so near to him but still out of reach.

As the sun approached the meridian that day it became insufferably warm. Its hot rays scorched the ground. The earth almost blistered the foot that stood upon it. I was without coat or hat, standing bare-headed, exposed to its burning blaze. Great drops of perspiration rolled down my face, drenching the scanty apparel wherewith I was clothed. Over the fence, a very little way off, the peach trees cast their cool, delicious shadows on the grass. I would gladly have given a long year of service to have been enabled to exchange the heated oven, as it were, wherein I stood, for a seat beneath their branches. But I was yet bound, the rope still dangling from my neck, and standing in the same tracks where Tibeats and his comrades left me. I could not move an inch, so firmly had I been bound. To have been enabled to lean against the weaving-house would have been a luxury indeed. But it was far beyond my reach, though

> The exaggerated image of the 'heated oven' confirms the intense heat.

ACTIVITY 2

Detailed references to parts of the body and 'swollen flesh' which is 'burying the rope'; I think this is a very graphic physical description.

distant less than twenty feet. I wanted to lie down, but knew I could not rise again. The ground was so parched and boiling hot I was aware it would but add to the discomfort of my situation. If I could only have moved my position, however slightly, it would have been a relief unspeakable. But the hot rays of the southern sun, beating all the long summer day on my bare head, produced not half the suffering I experienced from my aching limbs. My wrists and ankles, and the cords of my legs and arms began to swell, burying the rope that bound them into the swollen flesh.

Northrup changes focus from the heat to his uncomfortable position; he is desperately wishing he could adjust his posture, 'however slightly'.

ACTIVITY 3

You should begin your response to Component 2, Question 4 with a brief introduction: a summary statement presenting your personal judgement on the text (and, if relevant, how far you agree with the statement in the question).

What is your personal judgement on the *Twelve Years a Slave* extract in relation to the question? Do you think Northrup is successful in conveying his suffering and pain? Write no more than two sentences in the space provided.

....

....

....

....

EXAM TIP

Although you do need to evaluate the methods the writer uses for this question, you do not need to use subject terminology. Your focus should always be on answering the question and evaluating the text. Do not fall into the trap of feature-spotting.

How to write a Grade 5 response to this question

In your answer to Component 2, Question 4 you need to ensure that you:

- show you have a secure overall understanding of the text as a whole
- consider your own personal response to the text in relation to the question
- make detailed references to the text, including quotations
- explore and evaluate how the writer has written the text.

ACTIVITY 4

'Solomon Northup conveys his pain and suffering really well.' How far do you agree with this statement?

You should comment on:

■ what he says

■ how he says it.

a) Read the paragraph below. How could it be improved to a Grade 5 standard? Use the checklist to help you.

> **A** In this extract the writer is experiencing lots of pain and suffering. He is bound by rope and is unable to move. He is also standing in bright sunshine 'burning blaze'. The ropes used to bind him are digging into his skin. All of these things combined make it clear that Northup is experiencing pain and suffering.

Has this student:

■ shown they have a secure overall understanding of the text?

■ provided their own view in relation to the statement given in the question?

■ made quotations and provided detailed references to the text?

■ explored and evaluated how the writer has written the text?

b) Using the completed checklist above, write down a key piece of advice you would give this student in order to help them to achieve a Grade 5.

....

....

....

c) Read the Grade 5 paragraph B and accompanying annotations.

There are more specific references to the text than paragraph A. The quotations are concise and integrated into the sentences.

> **B** I think Solomon Northrup conveys his pain and suffering in powerful ways. For example, the passage begins with a vivid description of the intense heat he is forced to endure. He is exposed to the hot sun, which is described as a 'burning blaze'. The word 'burning' successfully emphasises the extent of the heat and suggests the pain he is feeling as a result. His suffering is made even worse because he is taunted by the

This is a clear point which relates specifically to the question. The student has used the first person ('I think') which is appropriate because the question is asking you to evaluate the text.

The student has successfully focused on a detail in the quotation ('burning') and has explained its effects in relation to the question.

ACTIVITY 4

> Clear and concise explanation of the effects of the adjectives.

sight of the contrasting 'cool, delicious shadows on the grass'. These adjectives emphasise the welcoming aspects of the shade. The shade is frustratingly just out of reach and I think this therefore helps to convey his suffering.

> The word 'contrasting' here is really effective because it shows the student is looking at how Northrup has structured the text. It develops the paragraph by comparing the presentation of the heat with the shade.

> This is a successful link to the statement in the question and provides a clear evaluation.

d) Read the Grade 5 paragraph C below. Annotate it with examples of the following:
- a clear point which relates specifically to the question
- specific references to the extract
- integrated quotations
- clear and relevant explanation of the effects of the quotation or method
- clear, personal evaluation of the statement in the question.

> **C** After describing suffering caused by the intense midday heat, Northrup then conveys the difficulties he experienced in being unable to move because he is painfully bound by rope. His 'wrist and ankles' and his 'legs and arms' begin to swell. The graphic image of the rope being buried by the 'swollen flesh' really conveys to me the pain he must be feeling. The verb 'burying' suggests that his arms are so swollen he can no longer see the rope which is binding him. I think this is a very gruesome image which successfully conveys Northrup's agony.

e) Using paragraphs B and C in the previous activities as models, write another paragraph in response to the same question. Use some of the annotations from Activities 1 and 2 to help you.

....

....

....

....

....

....

....

....

....

Extended practice

Read the text below and write a response to the example Component 2, Question 4 below. After reading the text, limit yourself to 12 minutes, which is how long you should spend answering this question in the exam.

Remember to consider and apply the skills covered in this chapter:

- Make sure you read the question and the text carefully.
- Remember to evaluate the text and develop your own personal response in relation to the question.
- Start with a brief opening paragraph which summarises your view on the text in relation to the question.
- Consider the effects of the language and structure of the passage in your response.
- Make sure you quote and provide detailed references to the text.

How successful do you think James Gleisher is in conveying his wonder at the view of London?

You should comment on:

- what he describes
- how he describes it.

You must refer to the text to support your comments.

In this extract the writer, James Gleisher, is describing a hot-air balloon trip over London. The extract is taken from his book Travels in the Air, *which was first published in 1871.*

On leaving Charing Cross I looked back over London, the model of which could be seen and traced – its squares by their lights; the river, which looked dark and dull, by the double row of lights on every bridge spanning it. Looking round, two of the illuminated dials of Westminster clock were like two dull moons. Again, looking eastward, the whole lines of the Commercial and Whitechapel roads, with their continuations through Holborn to Oxford Street, were visible, and most brilliant and remarkable. We were at such a distance from the Commercial Road that it appeared like a line of brilliant fire, assuming a more imposing appearance when the line separated into two, and most imposing just under us in Oxford Street. Here the two thickly-studded rows of brilliant lights were seen on either side of the street, with a narrow dark space between, and this dark space was bounded, as it were, on both sides by a bright fringe like frosted silver. At first I could not account for this appearance; but presently, at one point more brilliant than the rest, persons were seen passing, their shadows being thrown on the pavement, and at once it was evident this rich effect was caused by the brilliant illumination of the shop-lights on the pavements.

I feel it is impossible to convey any adequate idea of the brilliant effect of London, viewed at an elevation of 1,300 feet, on a clear night, when the air is free from mist.

It seemed to me to realize a wish I have felt when looking through a telescope at portions of the Milky Way, when the field of view appeared covered with gold-dust, to be possessed of the power to see those minute spots of light as brilliant stars; for certainly the intense brilliancy of London this night must have rivalled such a view.

CHECK YOUR PROGRESS

You have now practised the skills needed for a Grade 5 response to Component 2, Question 4.
Read your response to the Extended Practice task.
Did you:

	✔
Read the question and the text carefully?	
Read the question and the text carefully?	
Start with a brief opening paragraph which summarises your view on the text in relation to the question?	
Consider the effects of the language and structure of the passage in your response?	
Quote and provide detailed references to the text?	

Your reflections

Reflect on your answers and the progress check you completed. Which elements of Component 2, Question 4 do you feel more confident about? Which areas do you feel you still need to work on?

....

....

....

....

....

Question 5: Selecting and combining information from both texts

For Component 2, Question 5 you will be asked to find information from both non-fiction texts and to show your understanding by bringing this information together. This is known as **synthesis**.

There are four marks for this question. Aim to spend about five minutes answering it.

Example exam question

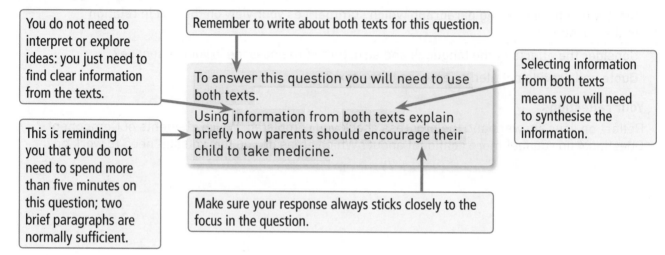

You do not need to interpret or explore ideas: you just need to find clear information from the texts.

Remember to write about both texts for this question.

Selecting information from both texts means you will need to synthesise the information.

To answer this question you will need to use both texts.

Using information from both texts explain briefly how parents should encourage their child to take medicine.

This is reminding you that you do not need to spend more than five minutes on this question; two brief paragraphs are normally sufficient.

Make sure your response always sticks closely to the focus in the question.

How do I achieve a Grade 5 response to this question?

You will need to satisfy the following criteria in order to achieve a Grade 5 for Component 2, Question 5:

- **Select** relevant information from both texts.
- Combine (**synthesise**) the information by writing about both texts together.
- Show a clear **understanding** of both texts.

> **EXAM TIP**
>
> Underline the key words and focus in the question before you begin preparing and writing your response.

This extract is taken from an NHS leaflet called 'Tips to help your child to take medicine'.

Convincing a child to take medicine can sometimes be a difficult task. Children often don't want to take medicine. This might be because they find it unpleasant or scary. They may also not understand why they have to take it. This leaflet aims to give you some tips on making the process easier for both you and your child.

Talking it through with your child

- Talk to your child and find out what is wrong; why do they not want to take the medicine? It is important that you acknowledge their fears (that it tastes horrible, etc.) as this help you to talk with them about how you can make it better.

- It is important that your child understands why they have to take the medicine and what could happen if they don't take it. However, don't try to scare your child into taking the medicine!

- Reassure your child that they are not having to take the medicine because they have been naughty.

- Be calm but firm and give your child honest explanations. Talk about it in a way that doesn't make your child feel like they are failing or letting you down.

Common reasons children won't take medicine

- not understanding why they need to take it
- not liking the taste or texture
- having difficulty swallowing tablets or capsules.

Giving the medicine

- Find out which way your child prefers to take the medicine, such as from a spoon, syringe, dropper, or drinking from a cup or straw. Ask them where they would like to be when they take the medicine (on your knee, on the sofa, in bed).
- Find out from your doctor whether liquid medicine can be mixed with food or liquid. It may taste nicer with a small amount of juice, honey or chocolate spread, or something else nice-tasting to wash it down. Do not dilute the medicine too much though or it may take you a long time to get your child to take it all.

This extract is taken from Babyhood, The Mother's Nursery Guide *(1898), which advises mothers on how to raise children.*

[W]ould it not be wise on the part of the mother, when her children are suffering from trifling ailments, to train them to take readily whatever may be necessary, so that when more serious troubles come they may find it easy to do so?

[When] we find it advisable to give some medicine to our children, do not let us make it a condition that it shall be perfectly unobjectionable in taste. Explain to the child the reason of your giving it. In answer to the almost invariable question, 'Is it nice, mother?' do not temporize; say at once, 'No, it is not nice; but I wish you to take it like a brave child.' By so doing we stimulate the will to do a brave deed, for to a child it is a brave deed …

What a source of strength it is for a mother to be able to say with confidence, in answer to the question whether one of her treasures could be induced to take a disagreeable drug, 'Yes; I am sure I can get him to take anything you order.' Children who are trained to behave reasonably during illness learn to look upon it with much less fear than those to whom it means a succession of battles. Its sorrows are more quickly forgotten, through the compensations in the way of entertainment during convalescence. They learn to look upon the physician and nurse as their friends, no less because they come in a time of trouble.

temporize: avoid making a decision

Selecting evidence

Using information from both texts, explain briefly how parents should encourage their child to take medicine.

You should read the question carefully and work out what the key words are. The example question above is asking you to explain how **parents should care for their sick child**. You should then select evidence that is relevant to the question from both texts.

ACTIVITY 1

To prepare for this question, a student selected the following quotations from the *Babyhood, The Mother's Nursery Guide* extract:

'train them to take readily whatever may be necessary'/'trained to behave reasonably'

'Explain to the child the reason of your giving it'

'stimulate the will to do a brave deed'

Read the NHS leaflet again. Select quotations which will help you to explain how parents should encourage their child to take medicine. Write them in the space provided below.

EXAM TIP

Make sure your response focuses on the question and that you select appropriate details. For this question, students can sometimes drift away from the topic and write about the text in a general way.

Synthesising the evidence

Once you have selected the evidence you need to respond to Component 2, Question 5, you need to combine (**synthesise**) the points in your answer.

1 Begin with an overview that sums up the point you are making.

2 Provide details and evidence from the first text.

3 As you move on to the second text, use a relevant comparative signpost, such as '**similarly**', '**likewise**' or '**on the other hand**'.

4 Then provide details and evidence from the second text.

Repeat Steps 1–4 with another point.

Read this Grade 5 paragraph and the accompanying annotations.

This overview uses key words from the question which indicate the answer is going to be relevant. 'Both writers' indicates that the student is synthesising the two texts.

Both writers advise parents to talk to their children when giving medicine and to explain what is happening and not keep them in the dark. The NHS leaflet says that it is 'important that your child understands why they have to take the medicine' and suggests that parents should clarify this to them. Similarly, the writer of Babyhood advises mothers to 'explain to the child' the reason why they are giving the medicine.

This comparative signpost again shows that the student is synthesising evidence from both texts.

Well-selected, relevant evidence from both texts.

ACTIVITY 2

a) Read the Grade 3 response below. Explain in the space provided how this student could improve the paragraph. Use the advice and guidance above to help you.

The writer of the NHS leaflet thinks parents should make efforts to make their children feel comfortable, such as asking them if they would prefer the medicine to be taken with 'a spoon, syringe, dropper, or drinking from a cup or straw'. The writer of Babyhood thinks children should be trained to do what their parents say and to behave in a reasonable way.

Three ways this paragraph could be improved are:

i Include an overview at the beginning to synthesise the texts, such as 'The writer of Babyhood thinks parents should be much firmer with children than the writer of the NHS leaflet'.

ii ....
....

iii ....
....

b) Now write another paragraph. You could re-work the Grade 3 paragraph above, or write your own. Remember to follow the advice given in this chapter.

....
....
....
....
....
....
....

> ## EXAM TIP
>
> Do not waste time copying out long titles and author's full names in the exam. When referring to each text in the exam, you could use instead:
>
> - the writer's **surnames** (if known)
> - the different **text types** (if different), such as the article, the biography, the journal
> - a shortened version of the title, for example, *Babyhood, The Mother's Nursery Guide* could be shortened to *Babyhood*.

Extended practice

Read the two texts on pages 68 and 69 and write a response to the accompanying example Component 2, Question 5. After reading the texts, limit yourself to five minutes, which is how long you should spend answering this question in the exam.

Remember to consider and apply the skills covered in this chapter:

- Read the texts and the question carefully.
- Select evidence from both texts in relation to the question.
- Synthesise the evidence from both texts by adopting the following process:
  - ☐ Begin each paragraph with an overview that sums up the point you are making.
  - ☐ Provide details and evidence from the first text.
  - ☐ As you move on to the second text use a comparative signpost, such as 'similarly', 'likewise' or 'on the other hand'.
  - ☐ Then provide details and evidence from the second text.
- Aim for two paragraphs.

Using information from both texts explain the experiences and attitudes of lifeboat volunteers.

This text is taken from an article for the Guardian *newspaper written by Mark King.*

A working life: The lifeboat volunteer

Mark Bell may not get paid for entering perilous waters – day or night – to perform rescues but, as he tells Mark King, the reward is knowing he has saved lives

Mark Bell is patiently trying to explain what sponsons are and how tidal flows work, but he keeps getting interrupted by a succession of friendly faces. 'It's busy today,' he smiles, acknowledging the obvious camaraderie on display among the lifeboat crew at Brighton's Royal National Lifeboat Institution (RNLI) station, 'but it's less noisy on a freezing night at 2am when we've had an emergency call from the coastguard.'

We're in a square brick building in Brighton marina which, at 51 hectares (127 acres), is one of the largest in Europe. The RNLI building was built 13 years ago with funds from a legacy donation left by a generous local lady. 'We're a charity that relies on donations and funding to maintain a service, so that was priceless,' Bell says …

Bell is a web developer who works from home and can therefore be on call 24/7. A crew diary is kept so everyone knows who is available at any given time. People who cannot get away from their jobs during the day make sure they are on call during the night. Either way, it's a huge commitment. 'It's an enormously rewarding thing to do, but it does become a huge part of your life and it can put an enormous strain on your family and employer,' Bell admits. So what motivates him to do the role – for free? 'In Brighton our busiest months are generally May to September, when the beaches are busier and the marina berth holders head out to sea. But, like many of us, I do it for the winter months when the incidents tend to be a little more serious and the conditions are fairly unpleasant. At 2am in a freezing February storm we are likely to be able to make a much more profound difference on the outcome of an incident.'

The crew begin to gather in a large communal area with a 270-degree view of the marina, sea and coastline, and banter like any group of close friends who work and socialise together. They chat excitedly while throwing me curious but friendly glances. Bell explains that there is little laughing or joking when a call goes out.

'On a launch everyone is on autopilot and there's no idle chit-chat. We're all establishing the facts: the location and condition of any casualties, while also rushing to the boat and launching into the water. The first few minutes are intense.'

This extract is taken from an article in Household Words *(1857) by Charles Dickens. The extract describes the life of 'hovellers', who crew lifeboats on the coast of Kent.*

It is a dark night in December, and it blows a gale of wind. The hovelling world of **Broadstairs** is on the alert, for somebody has heard a gun, and it is expected that a ship is on shore in the **Godwin Sands**.

Some five-and-twenty men, all **hovellers**, are now congregated on the pier. Both lifeboats are in readiness, and so are the three **luggers**. How impatiently some of the men walk to and fro! That tall and strongly-built man with the handsome features and open countenance is old Jem Taylor. If asked to guess his age, you would say five-and-forty; but to my knowledge he is over sixty-six. He served his thirty years in the Royal Navy, and was a **quartermaster** for twenty-two years of the period. He is now an out-pensioner of Greenwich Hospital, and draws his twenty-nine pounds per annum. There is scarcely a port in the world that he has not visited – East and West Indies, China, South America, Africa, Australia. He has served in fourteen of Her Majesty's ships, and from every captain has a certificate that his conduct was very good, and that he was always obedient to command. Taylor has seen some hard fighting in his day, and wears upon his Sunday jacket several silver medals; but the medal of which he seems the most proud is the one awarded him for saving life.

If you ask why, at his time of life, and now that he is provided for by his pension, he engages in the dangerous business of hovelling, he will tell you that he feels a young man still; that he likes the life of adventure, and that idleness would drive him mad.

Broadstairs: a coastal town in Kent

Godwin Sands: a sandbank (a bank of sand just below the surface of the sea) off the coast in Kent; in this extract, they fear a ship has been wrecked on the sandbank

hovellers: boatmen on the coast of Kent

luggers: a small sailing ship

quartermaster: the person who steers a ship in the Royal Navy

CHECK YOUR PROGRESS

You have now practised the skills needed for a Grade 5 response to Component 2, Question 5. Read through your response to the Extended Practice task and identify where you have satisfied the criteria for a Grade 5. Complete the table by ticking the statements which apply to your response.

	✔
I wrote two paragraphs.	
I began each paragraph with an overview that summed up the point I was making.	
I selected evidence from both texts.	
The evidence I selected was relevant to the focus in the question ('the experiences and attitudes of lifeboat volunteers').	
I used comparative signposts such as 'both writers', 'similarly', 'on the other hand'.	

Your reflection

Are there any statements you did not tick? If so, how can you make sure you include these features in future responses?

....

....

....

....

Question 6: Comparing texts

Component 2, Question 6 assesses your ability to **compare** both texts. You need to write about the writers' ideas and perspectives on a particular subject. You will need to explain and compare how the ideas and perspectives are conveyed through the writers' choices of language, structure and other methods.

The question is worth ten marks. You should aim to spend about 12–15 minutes answering the question.

Example exam question

This is the key command word. You need to compare both texts by exploring the similarities and differences. Avoid writing about one text and then the other.

You need to show an understanding of what the writers have to say about the topic in the question and how they are similar or different. This is known as 'ideas and perspectives' and is explained in more detail in the activities in this chapter.

Remember this is a comparison question so you need to write equally about both texts.

Both of these texts contain accounts of travel.
Compare:
- what the writers say about their encounters
- how the writers get across their experience to the reader.

You must use the text to support your comment and make it clear which text you are referring to.

This part of the question will indicate the topic or subject both texts have in common. Make sure all your points relate clearly to this focus.

You also need to show an understanding of the methods used by the writers, such as tone, structure or use of language, and how they are similar or different.

This is reminding you that you need to quote and refer to textual details in your answer.

You can do this by referring to the title or the writers of the text. It might sometimes be necessary to use a shorter version of the title.

How do I achieve a Grade 5 in my response to this question?

You will need to satisfy the following criteria in order to achieve a Grade 5 for Component 2, Question 6:
- Clearly compare relevant ideas and perspectives.
- Explain clearly how writers' methods are used.
- Select quotations and details from both texts.
- Show a clear understanding of the different perspectives and ideas in both texts.

EXAM TIP

Students often run out of time for this question and produce short and under-developed responses as a result. Keep an eye on the clock in the exam and make sure you are disciplined with your timings for the previous questions.

Identifying writers' ideas and perspectives

Both texts in Component 2 will share a common subject, for example, prisons or riding a hot-air balloon or hunting. You will need to work out the writers' opinions or attitudes towards the subject in both texts. This is called identifying writers' ideas and perspectives.

ACTIVITY ①

Read the extract from *Dark Star Safari*. As you read, consider the questions on the writer's ideas and perspectives. When you have finished reading, write your answers in the space provided.

This extract is taken from Dark Star Safari: Overland from Cairo to Capetown, *a travel book written by Paul Theroux. In this extract, the writer is travelling in a cattle truck into Kenya in Africa. He has been warned that the journey will take him into a dangerous area where trucks are frequently attacked by armed bandits (known locally as* shifta*).*

I was calm, even happy. I wrapped my jacket around me to protect me from the dust and watched the suffering cattle. Weak from thirst, tottering from the movement of the truck, slumping to their knees and now and then knocked to the truck bed, they were getting smacked in the chops and their tails twisted. I could hear their pained mooing over the chunking of the wheels on the road.

Deep in the desert were the camel trains of the **Borena**, pure panic cloaked in beauty, the yellow robed women walking ahead, the men guiding the camels. It was a lovely sight and yet it was a matter of life or death, illustrating the desperate need for water. No rain, no nearby wells; so the camel train went a great distance and returned laden with jerry cans and drums of water. Each camel was covered in heavy tin containers, slopping the animals' shanks.

I had to hold tight to stay upright on the truck. The road was not only rocky but here, it ceased to go straight – it wound between huge humps, too small to be hills, but obstructions all the same. We went very slowly. I could not see ahead. I was relieved that, as we were moving so slowly, I did not have to cling so tightly.

Then I heard a loud bang, and thought: Oh, no, a **blowout**. But another bang followed it, and the men on top pushed past me to dive into the mass of groaning cattle.

I got a glimpse of two men in dusty robes, their faces hidden by bands of cloth, standing in the road, with rifles held upright, firing into the air.

Two things happened then. First, and startlingly, the man crouched beside me – a soldier – lifted his rifle and began firing directly at the men, both of whom ducked behind boulders. Second, the truck accelerated, moving so fast that it pitched and rolled down the narrow defile between the humpy hills, like a toppling yacht traveling down the face of a wave.

And at the same time, I was diving down from the top bars of the truck with the other men, and dangling behind the metal sides (thinking, *Is this steel bulletproof?*) and over the staggering cattle. We went from five to twenty-five miles an hour, not great acceleration perhaps but enough to drag us out of range of the armed men and to demonstrate our resolve to get away.

The men were *shifta*, classic highwaymen positioned in a perfect place. The truck had slowed down to a crawl in a spot that was squeezed between two hiding places, and the men stepped out and fired in the air to get our attention. Perhaps they had not counted on being fired upon; more likely they were surprised by the driver stamping on the gas and getting us out of there.

The soldier clinging to the bars beside me on our truck shook his head and laughed.

I said, '*Shifta*?'

'Yah.' He smiled at my grim face.

I said, '*Sitaki kufa*,' I don't want to die.

He said in English, 'They don't want your life, **bwana**. They want your shoes.'

Many times after that, in my meandering through Africa, I mumbled these words, an **epitaph** of underdevelopment, desperation in a single sentence. What use is your life to them? It is nothing. But your shoes – ah, they are a different matter, they are worth something, much more than your watch (they had the sun) or your pen (they were illiterate) or your bag (they had nothing to put in it). These were men who needed footwear, for they were forever walking.

ACTIVITY 1

Borena: an ethnic group who live in southern Ethiopia and northern Kenya

blowout: a burst tyre

bwana: boss or master

epitaph: words by which something will be remembered

a) Although Theroux feels calm and happy in the first paragraph, what does he think about the cattle in the truck?

....

....

....

b) Although Theroux says the camel trains of the Borena people are beautiful, why are they actually a 'matter of life and death'? What do we learn about the lives of the Borena in the second paragraph?

....

....

....

c) How do we know that the road is dangerous? How did Theroux manage to get away unhurt?

....

....

....

d) 'They don't want your life, *bwana*. They want your shoes.' What do we learn about the bandits' way of life in the final paragraph? What are Theroux's opinions towards his attackers?

....

....

....

ACTIVITY 2

Look again at your answers to the questions in Activity 1. Summarise in your own words Theroux's ideas and perspectives about the area and his journey.

....

....

....

....

ACTIVITY ③

Read the extract below. When you have finished reading, write your answers in the space provided.

This extract is taken from Through the Dark Continent *(1878) by Henry Morton Stanley, a Victorian explorer. The book is an account of an expedition along the course of the Congo river in Africa. In this extract, Morton Stanley is describing an encounter with a tribe as his expedition travels down the river.*

In these wild regions our mere presence excited the most furious passions of hate and murder, just as in shallow waters a deep vessel stirs up muddy sediments. It appeared to be a necessity, then why should we regret it? Could a man contend with the inevitable?

… We pull briskly on to gain the right bank, and come in view of the right branch of the **affluent**, when, looking upstream, we see a sight that sends the blood tingling through every nerve and fibre of the body, arouses not only our most lively interest, but also our lively apprehensions – a **flotilla** of gigantic canoes bearing down upon us, which both in size and numbers utterly eclipse anything encountered hitherto! Instead of aiming for the right bank, we form a line, and keep straight down the river, the boat taking position behind. Yet after a moment's reflection, as I note the numbers of savages, and the daring manner of the pursuit, and the desire of our canoes to abandon the steady compact line, I give the order to drop anchor …

We have sufficient time to take a view of the mighty force bearing down on us, and to count the number of war-vessels which have been collected from the Livingstone and its great affluent. There are fifty-four of them! A monster canoe leads the way, with two rows of upstanding paddles, forty men on a side, their bodies bending and swaying in unison as with a swelling **barbarous** chorus they drive her down towards us. In the bow, standing on what appears to be a platform, are ten prime young warriors, their heads [bright] with feathers of the parrot, crimson and grey: at the stern, eight men, with long paddles, whose tops are decorated with ivory balls, guide the monster vessel; and dancing up and down from stern to stern are ten men, who appears to be chiefs. All the paddles are headed with ivory balls, every head bears a feather crown, every arm shows gleaming white ivory armlets. From the bow of the canoe streams a thick fringe of the long white fibre of the **Hyphene palm**. The crashing sound of large drums, a hundred blasts from ivory horns, and a thrilling chant from two thousand human throats, do not tend to soothe our nerves or to increase our confidence. However, it is '**neck or nothing**.' We have no time to pray, or to take sentimental looks at the savage world, or even breathe a sad farewell to it. So many other things have to be done speedily and well.

As the foremost canoe comes rushing down, and its consorts on either side beating the water into foam, and raising their jets of water with their sharp prows, I turn to take a last look at our people, and say to them:

'Boys, be firm as iron; wait until you see the first spear and then take good aim. Don't fire all at once. Keep aiming until you are sure of your man. Don't think of running away, for only your guns can save you.'

… Our blood is up now. It is a murderous world, and we feel for the first time that we hate the filthy, vulturous ghouls who inhabit it.

affluent: a river or stream that flows into a larger river

flotilla: a fleet of boats

barbarous: brutal and uncivilised

Hyphene palm: a variety of palm tree

'**neck or nothing**': an attempt at success that risks losing everything

ACTIVITY 3

a) In the first paragraph, Morton Stanley reflects on how he should respond to the 'passions of hate and murder' his presence has created in the area. Summarise his view on how he should respond in your own words.

....

....

....

b) How and why does Morton Stanley try to make his account exciting and dramatic?

....

....

....

c) What do you notice about the way the men are described in the third paragraph?

....

....

....

d) What are Morton Stanley's opinions towards the people who live in the area he is exploring?

....

....

....

ACTIVITY 4

Look again at your answers to the questions in Activity 3. Summarise in your own words Morton Stanley's ideas and perspectives about the area and his encounter.

....

....

....

....

....

Comparing ideas and perspectives

Both of these texts contain accounts of encounters in Africa.

Compare:

- what the writers say about their encounters
- how the writers get across their experience to the reader.

The first bullet point in the question reminds you that you need to think about the similarities and differences between the ideas and attitudes of both writers. You can use these differences and similarities to help you to structure your points.

EXAM TIP

Perhaps more so than the other Reading questions, you need to spend some time planning your response for Question 6. Think about the points of comparisons – similarities and differences – and sketch these out before you begin.

ACTIVITY 5

Use your answers to Activities 1–4 to help you complete the comparison table below. Once you have completed the table, you will be able to see the range of differences and similarities you could explore in a response to this question.

Theroux, *Dark Star Safari*	Similarity or difference?	Henry Morton Stanley, *Through the Dark Continent*
Point: Theroux has sympathy for the Borena people, who have to travel great distances for water. **Detail:** 'it was a matter of life or death, illustrating the desperate need for water'	**Difference**	**Point:** Morton Stanley sees the people in the area as inevitably murderous. **Detail:** 'the most furious passions of hate and murder'
Point: Theroux has a violent, frightening encounter. **Detail:**	**Similarity**	**Point:** Morton Stanley has a violent, frightening encounter. **Detail:** 'The crashing sound of large drums, a hundred blasts from ivory horns, and a thrilling chant from two thousand human throats, do not tend to soothe our nerves'
Point: The violence in Dark Star Safari happens very quickly and is out of the blue. **Detail:**	**Difference**	**Point:** Morton Stanley provides detailed description of the build up to the violence. **Detail:**

ACTIVITY 5

Theroux, *Dark Star Safari*	Similarity or difference?	Henry Morton Stanley, *Through the Dark Continent*
Point: Theroux has some sympathy for the bandits who attack him. **Detail:**	**Difference**	**Point:** **Detail:**
Point: **Detail:**	**A further difference or similarity of your own**	**Point:** **Detail:**

EXAM TIP

Note how the points in this table 'track through' both texts, rather than just focussing on one section. Make sure your references and quotations are from across the whole text for this question.

ACTIVITY 6

a) Read this paragraph taken from a student's response to this question. Read also the accompanying annotations. The student has based their response on the first row in the table in Activity 5. The paragraph has all the hallmarks of a Grade 5 response.

A clear comparison of the ideas in both texts

Clear, relevant textual detail

Concise explanation of quotations

> Theroux has sympathy for the people who live in the area whereas Morton Stanley sees the people as excessively violent. Theroux writes that the Borena people in the camel train are fetching water as 'a matter of life or death' and how they are in 'desperate' need of water. The word 'desperate' suggests Theroux has sympathy for the people around him and that their lives must be very difficult. On the other hand, Morton Stanley describes the people around him as having 'the most furious passions of hate and murder'. This indicates that he sees them as violent and that it is in their nature because he describes their hatred as 'inevitable'.

The student uses the writers' names to make it clear which text they are writing about.

Clear comparative signpost as the student moves from one text to another

ACTIVITY (6)

b) How could this Grade 3 paragraph be improved? Look at the Grade 5 paragraph and annotations to help you.

> The writer has a violent, frightening encounter. He saw two men 'with rifles held upright, firing into the air.' This would be very shocking for the writer. In the other text, the writer has a frightening encounter. 'The crashing sound of large drums, a hundred blasts from ivory horns, and a thrilling chant from two thousand human throats, do not tend to soothe our nerves'. The really loud sounds make him feel even more frightened.

This paragraph could be improved in the following three ways:

i ....

....

ii ....

....

iii ....

....

c) Look at the table you completed in Activity 5. Take one point and supporting detail from the Theroux column and compare it with a point and supporting detail from the Morton Stanley column. Do not use the first row.

Using the paragraph in Activity 6 a) as a model, write another comparative paragraph below.

....

....

....

....

....

....

....

....

EXAM TIP

Your reading and ideas for Questions 1–5 are good preparation for this question. By the time you get to Question 6, you should have a good understanding of both texts. Don't worry too much about repeating some points or quotations from previous responses: just make sure you are always answering the question.

Comparing methods

The second bullet point in the question will remind you that you need to compare the methods the writers use. Depending on the texts you are given in the exam, you could consider some or all of the following:

■ persuasive devices
■ language choices and imagery
■ structure
■ tone.

There are three ways to include a comparison of methods in your response:

1 You could explore methods as part of your **comparison of the ideas and perspectives** of the two texts. For example:

> Theroux has sympathy for the people who live in the area **whereas** Morton Stanley sees the people as excessively violent. Theroux writes that the Borena people in the camel train are fetching water as 'a matter of life or death' and how 'desperately' they need water. The adjective 'desperate' suggests Theroux has sympathy for the people around him and that their lives must be very difficult. On the other hand, Morton Stanley describes the people around him as having 'the most furious passions of hate and murder'. The adjective 'most furious' indicates that he sees them as violent and that it is in their nature because he describes their hatred as 'inevitable'.

2 You could make **a comparative point on the methods** themselves. For example, you could identify similar language or structural techniques in both texts and then explain the different effects they create.
For example:

> **Both writers** use metaphors to describe the people they encounter. Theroux describes the Borena people as 'pure panic cloaked in beauty'. This sympathetically suggests that, although the Borena people are pleasing to look at, this actually disguises their desperate search for water. Morton Stanley, **in contrast**, uses a metaphor to describe the people he encounters as cruel and monstrous: 'filthy, vulturous ghouls'.

3 You could write about how **tones are created differently** in the two texts.
For example:

> **Both writers** adopt a dramatic and exciting tone to describe the events they experience. Theroux uses exciting verbs as he describes himself 'diving down' and 'dangling behind the metal sides' as he hears the gunshots. Theroux panics and tries to hide. **On the other hand**, Morton Stanley uses the rule of three when describing the sounds he can hear: 'The crashing sound of large drums, a hundred blasts from ivory horns, and a thrilling chant from two thousand human throats'. The writer is really emphasising the suspense as the noises get louder. He is perhaps also suggesting how brave and excited he is because he does not run away from the danger.

ACTIVITY 7

a) Draw a line to match the methods to the quotations taken from *Dark Star Safari* on page 72.

Quotation		Method
tottering, slumping, knocked, smacked		Metaphor
pure panic cloaked in beauty		Repetition
No rain, no nearby wells		Verbs
startlingly		Simile
He smiled at my grim face	→	Contrast
like a toppling yacht traveling down the face of a wave		Rule of three
He said in English, 'They don't want your life, *bwana*. They want your shoes.'		Dialogue
much more than your watch (they had the sun) or your pen (they were illiterate) or your bag (they had nothing to put in it)		Adverb

b) Which methods is Morton Stanley using in these quotations from *Through the Dark Continent* (page 74)? You may find more than one method in each quotation.

It appeared to be a necessity, then why should we regret it? Could a man contend with the inevitable?

Method(s) used: ....

....

A monster canoe leads the way

Method(s) used: ....

....

The crashing sound of large drums, a hundred blasts from ivory horns, and a thrilling chant from two thousand human throats

Method(s) used: ....

....

'Boys, be firm as iron; wait until you see the first spear and then take good aim …'

Method(s) used: ....

....

the filthy, vulturous ghouls

Method(s) used: ....

....

ACTIVITY 7

c) Look at your answers to Activity 7 a) and b). Do Theroux and Morton Stanley use any similar methods? List them below.

....

....

....

d) For Component 2, Question 6 you could consider comparing how the writers have **structured** the texts. Look at how Theroux and Morton Stanley have **ended** the texts. What similarities and/or differences do you notice?

....

....

....

....

ACTIVITY 8

a) Here is a paragraph from a Grade 5 response. Annotate the paragraph to indicate where the student has

- made a clear comparison of method in the opening
- used relevant textual details
- signposted the comparison
- written about the methods used by both writers.

> Both writers use metaphors to describe the people they encounter. Theroux describes the Borena people as 'pure panic cloaked in beauty'. This metaphor sympathetically suggests that, although the Borena people are pleasing to look at, this actually disguises their desperate search for water in order to stay alive. Morton Stanley, in contrast, uses a metaphor to describe the people he encounters as cruel and monstrous: 'filthy, vulturous ghouls'. He does not like or understand the people he encounters.

b) Read through this paragraph, taken from a Grade 3 response to the same question. A teacher has marked the paragraph and asked questions to prompt the student to think about how the paragraph could be improved. Answer the questions in the space provided on the next page.

ACTIVITY 8

i This opening sentence is clear and is directly relevant to the question. How could you make this opening sentence more comparative?

ii This is a relevant and accurate quotation to support your point. More detail would help, though: what specifically is being described as being 'like a toppling yacht'?

Theroux uses a simile to make the reader share the drama and suspense of his encounter in Africa: 'like a toppling yacht traveling down the face of a wave'. The other writer uses a simile as he instructs his companions to be 'as firm as iron'. The writer wants to show how brave he is – and how brave he expects others to be – as they encounter the fearsome warriors.

iii How can you make it clearer which text you are writing about?

iv What should you try to include in your paragraph as you move on to the second text?

v This is clear and thoughtful analysis of the method used here. How could you compare this with Theroux's attitude?

i

ii

iii

iv

v

ACTIVITY 8

c) Using your answers to Activity 8 a) and b), write at least one further comparative paragraph of your own. Make sure you compare the **methods** used (**how** the writers get across their experience to the reader).
Here is the question again to remind you:

> Both of these texts contain accounts of encounters in Africa.
> Compare:
> - what the writers say about their encounters
> - how the writers get across their experience to the reader.

....

....

....

....

....

....

....

....

....

....

....

Extended practice

Read the two texts on pages 84–85 and write a response to the example Component 2, Question 6 below. After reading the texts, limit yourself to 12–15 minutes, which is how long you should spend answering this question in the exam.

Remember to consider and apply the skills covered in this chapter:
- Work out the writers' ideas and perspectives regarding the topic in the question.
- Compare the ideas and perspectives – are there any differences or similarities in their attitudes and opinions?
- Select relevant textual details.
- Compare the methods both writers use – are there any differences or similarities in the methods used or their effects?
- Structure your paragraph with a clear comparison at the beginning and clear comparative signposts as you move from one text to another.

> Both of these texts are about a prisoner's experiences in prison.
> Compare:
> - what the writers say about prison
> - how the writers get across their experiences to the reader.

This extract is taken from A Prison Diary *by Jeffrey Archer. On 19 July 2001, Jeffrey Archer, a former politician, was sentenced to four years in prison. He was to spend the first three weeks in HMP Belmarsh, a high security prison.*

Day 5 Monday 23 July 2001

5.53 am

The sun is shining through the bars of my window on what must be a glorious summer day. I've been incarcerated in a cell five paces by three for twelve and a half hours, and will not be let out again until midday; eighteen and a half hours of solitary confinement. There is a child of seventeen in the cell below me who has been charged with shoplifting - his first offence, not even convicted - and he is being locked up for eighteen and a half hours, unable to speak to anyone. This is Great Britain in the twenty-first century, not Turkey, not Nigeria, not Kosovo, but Britain.

I can hear the **right-wingers** assuring us that it will be character-building and teach the lad a lesson. What stupidity. It's far more likely that he will become antagonistic towards authority and once he's released, turn to a life of crime. This same young man will now be spending at least a fortnight with murderers, rapists, burglars and drug addicts. Are these the best tutors he can learn from?

12 noon

I am visited by a charming lady who spotted me sitting in church on Sunday. I end up asking her more questions than she asks me. It turns out that she visits every prisoner who signs the pledge - I fear I didn't - and any inmate who attends chapel for the first time. She gives each prisoner a Bible and will sit and listen to their problems for hours. She kindly answers all my questions. When she leaves, I pick up my plastic tray, plastic bowl, plastic plate, plastic knife, fork and spoon, leave my cell to walk down to the hotplate for lunch.

One look at what's on offer and once again I return to my cell empty-handed. An **old lag** on his way back to the top floor tells me that Belmarsh has the worst grub of any jail in Britain. As he's been a resident of seven prisons during the past twenty years, I take his word for it. An officer slams my cell door closed. It will not open again until four o'clock. I've had precisely twelve minutes of freedom during the last twenty-two and a half hours.

right-wingers: politicians who believe, amongst other things, that society should be tough on prisoners

old lag: a person who has been in prison many times

This extract is taken from an article first published in Household Words *magazine in 1853. It is written by an anonymous prisoner. In this extract, he is describing his first day at Newgate Gaol.*

Strong and stony as the prison seems to passers by, it looks much stonier and stronger to the men who enter it. The multiplicity of heavy walls, iron gates and doorways; of huge locks, of bolts, spikes and bars of every imaginable shape and size, make of the place a very nightmare dungeon. I followed the gruff under-warden, through some dark and chilly vaulted passages, now turning to the right, now to the left. We crossed a large hall, in the centre of which is a glass room for the use of prisoners when they are giving instructions to their lawyers.

Still following, I was led into another large recess or chamber, on one side of which was a huge boiler with a furnace glowing under it, and on another side a large stone bath. On the third wall there were a couple of round towels on a roller, with a wooden bench beneath them.

'Stop,' cried the warden, 'take your clothes off.' I hesitated. 'Take off your clothes, do you hear?' My clothes were soon laid on the bench, and a hot bath filled, and I went in. The officer then had his opportunity of taking up my garments one by one, searching their pockets and their linings, feeling them about and holding them against the light. My boots appeared to be especially suspicious. After he had put his hands into them, he thumped them violently on the stone floor; but there rolled nothing out.

Having bathed, I was led down another passage, at the end of which were two gratings of iron bars, closely woven over with wire-work, distant about two feet from each other. Unlocking both he pushed me through, and started up two or three steps into a square court-yard, where there was a man walking to and fro very violently. After shouting 'One in!' he locked the two gratings, and retreated rapidly in the direction of his dinner. Another warden with a bunch of keys came from a gloomy building that formed one side of the court. 'Go up,' he said to the pedestrian; who disappeared up the staircase instantly.

'Where are you from?' the jailor asked me, and 'What are you here for?' Being replied to on these points, he said shortly, 'Come this way.' He led up the dark stone staircase to a corridor with cells on one side, having iron doors to them a foot or more in thickness. One of those cells was to be mine.

CHECK YOUR PROGRESS

You have now practised the skills needed for Component 2, Question 6. Read through your answers to the Extended Practice question. Use different coloured pens to highlight sections of your answers which show you have achieved the criteria in the table below.

Then tick the statements which apply to your answers.

	✔
I have a clear overall understanding of both texts.	
My response is relevant to the focus in the question.	
I have a clear understanding of the writers' ideas and perspectives about their first day in prison.	
I have a clear understanding of the methods used by both writers.	
I can select relevant quotations and details from the text.	
I can clearly compare the writers' ideas and perspectives.	
I can clearly compare the writers' methods.	

CHECK YOUR PROGRESS

Your reflections

Reflect on your answers and the progress check you completed. Which elements of these questions do you feel more confident about? Which areas do you feel you still need to work on?

....

....

....

....

....

Component 1, Section B: Writing

Component 1 writing section: Creative prose writing

This section of the exam will assess the skill of writing creatively. You will choose one creative writing task from a choice of four. You will need to narrate or describe in an engaging way. You will also be assessed on the accuracy of your grammar, punctuation and spelling. (See Chapter 13 in this workbook for ways you can improve the accuracy of your writing.)

This task is worth 40 marks. You should spend ten minutes planning and 35 minutes writing and checking.

Example creative writing tasks

You are not required to write pages and pages for this task. Two or three pages of clear, well-planned and creative prose writing is normally sufficient.

Remember you only need to complete **one** task from the four.

One task might give you the **first line** of the story and you continue from there. The line normally gives a hint about what will or could happen next in the story.

You should aim to write about 450–600 words.

Choose one of the following titles for your writing:

Either:

a) Continue the following: I could tell from the moment I woke up that it was going to be a very bad day indeed.

OR

b) The Park Bench.

OR

c) Write about a time when you helped somebody.

OR

d) Write a story which ends: I haven't been on my bike ever since.

One task might give you the **final line** of the story and you need to plan and write your piece to lead up to this final line.

Another task might simply be a **short title** as a prompt for your creative response.

This task is guiding you to some **personal writing**, perhaps based in whole or in part on a memory or personal experience.

EXAM TIP

Avoid spending too long deciding on the writing task. You could consider choosing the task for which you can instantly think of plenty of good ideas. You may also have discovered in your English lessons that you write better responses for a particular type of task (such as personal writing) rather than another.

How do I achieve a Grade 5 in my response to this task?

You will need to satisfy the following criteria in order to achieve a Grade 5 for the writing section of Component 1:

- You need to communicate your ideas clearly and effectively.
- Your writing needs to be clearly matched to the task you have chosen.
- You need to use individual words, phrases and methods to impact your readers.
- You will need to organise your whole piece of writing, and the paragraphs within it.

You will also need to write accurately by meeting the following criteria:

- Use a range of vocabulary.
- Spell most words correctly, including some complex and sophisticated words.
- Write in correctly punctuated sentences.
- Use a variety of sentences to achieve specific effects.
- Write in Standard English.

Chapter 13 will focus on how to improve the accuracy of your writing.

What is a narrative?

Most responses to the writing task in Component 1 will take the form of a story or narrative. A narrative is normally based on a series of events. A narrative can be true and based on your own experience or it could be an imaginative story of your own invention or it could be a combination of the two.

Most stories will have:

- a well-described setting
- an event or events which engage the reader
- believable or interesting characters.

ACTIVITY 1

a) Re-read the following three extracts:

- the extract beginning 'When they reached the other side' from *The Silent Companions* by Laura Purcell (pages 14–15)
- the extract beginning 'I hope you're not bringing anything into the house that will smell?' from *Small Island* by Andrea Levy (pages 20–21)
- the extract beginning 'When they began to make their way along the front line trench' from *Strange Meeting* by Susan Hill (pages 27–28).

b) Complete the following table by summarising in your own words the setting, interesting or significant events and anything you learn about the main character(s).

	Setting	Interesting or significant events	What you learn about the main character(s)
The Silent Companions			

ACTIVITY (1)

	Setting	Interesting or significant events	What you learn about the main character(s)
Small Island			
Strange Meeting			

EXAM TIP

You should try to use the extracts you are given in this workbook, in your lessons and in the exam as models of good writing. They could give you ideas and inspiration for your own writing. You could also look at how they have structured their writing and other methods they use to make their story engaging.

Planning and structuring your response

You need to plan a narrative that introduces and develops the three important features:

- events
- setting
- character.

EXAM TIP

The tasks will provide you with a clear written prompt so you should always link your planned ideas to this.

A useful way to structure a narrative that includes these elements is as follows:

1 Establish setting and character
Try to locate your character(s) in a specific setting. This could be a good opportunity to use some effective creative writing techniques such as imagery and adjectives.

2 A complication
An event can take place that relates to the central character(s) in some way.

3 A development or consequence
The complicating event should then have a consequence or effect on the characters.

4 The ending
There is a conclusion or ending to the events.

A student has produced a plan for task d) on page 86:

Write a story which ends: I haven't been on my bike ever since.

1 Establish setting and character
Three boys riding their bikes along country lanes on a bright, sunny day. The narrator is younger and wants to impress the two older riders.

2 A complication
The narrator manages to get in front to show them he can ride with no hands down a hill.

3 A development or consequence
The narrator falls off and breaks his bike. The older boys laugh and cycle on without him. He walks alone, a long way from home, in the heat.

4 The ending
The bike remains broken. The narrator doesn't want to fix it because he is so embarrassed by what happened. This is why he hasn't been on his bike ever since.

EXAM TIP

Keep the events in your story simple and make sure your response isn't weighed down by a complicated plot or too many characters. In this example, the events are minimal and simple: a boy falls off his bike; his friends ride away and leave him.

ACTIVITY 2

a) Now plan your own response to this task: **'Write about a time when you helped somebody.'** Use the structure outlined above. Use the student example to help you as well.

1 Establish setting and character

....

....

....

2 A complication

....

....

....

3 A development or consequence

....

....

....

ACTIVITY 2

4 The ending

....

....

....

b) Now plan another response to this prompt: **'The Park Bench'**

1 Establish setting and character

....

....

....

2 A complication

....

....

....

3 A development or consequence

....

....

....

4 The ending

....

....

....

Beginning your narrative

The beginning and ending of your creative prose writing are very important. The beginning will need to hook the reader in to the story and make them want to read on.

You could begin your response with one of the following:

1 A vivid description

For example:

The summer sun flickered and danced between the trees as I raced down the hill on my bike. These verbs, and the personification of 'danced' help to establish the narrator's joy and to vividly set the scene.

2 A mystery

For example:

Something happened to me last year. Something incredibly embarrassing. Something which made me promise to myself I would never ride my bike again.

This student has deliberately withheld information and the mystery will really intrigue the reader. Note also the effective use of the rule of three.

3 Dialogue

For example:

'Watch me,' Eddie said as he lifted both arms and both legs away from the bike as he sped away down the hill.

'Show off,' Harry called, but he carefully watched Eddie accelerate towards the dangerous curve at the bottom of the hill.

This short dialogue exchange lets the reader hear the characters' voices and quickly establishes a relationship between Eddie and Harry.

4 An exciting or interesting action or event

For example:

I was pedalling as fast as I could, but Eddie easily cycled away from me, swerving dangerously towards the middle of the road.

This student has thrown the reader into the middle of the action. Excitement is established by Eddie swerving dangerously.

ACTIVITY 3

Look again at your response to Activity 2 a). Practise different ways of opening your narrative, using the examples provided above to help you.

1 A vivid description

....

....

....

2 A mystery

....

....

....

3 Dialogue

....

....

....

4 An exciting or interesting action or event

....

....

....

Characterisation

Creating clear and convincing character or characters can often help to make your narrative more engaging.

These features can help you to create character:

- thoughts and feelings
- action
- dialogue
- physical description.

ACTIVITY 4

Read the following extract from Susan Hill's novel *Strange Meeting*. The novel is set in the First World War.

In the officer's dining room, which had been the old dining room of the farmhouse and still retained the long refectory table, the light was better, he [Hilliard] could see Barton clearly. He did not seem like a man who would ever attract dislike. He was not quite twenty, and he looked older because he was mature, in complete possession of himself. It was not the premature ageing that often came to those who had been a short time at the front. He had some kind of natural poise and calmness. But all around that, on the surface, nothing was calm or still, he talked easily and quickly, smiled, laughed at himself and, on all sides, attracted a response …

He found himself watching Barton, listening, he felt drawn into the circle of his attention. He was talking about some relative, an aunt, who dashed about the Warwickshire countryside on a horse, riding astride not side-saddle, wearing breeches not skirts, to the horror of all who met her. She was called Eustacia.

'Only we none of us could ever say it properly, we all called her You-Stay-Shy. We still do.'

We?

Barton was cutting a wedge of cheese. He looked up for a moment, catching Hilliard's eye. His own were a curious green-blue, under a low forehead and thick, black hair. His voice was still full of amusement.

a) Highlight the extract to show how the writer presents the character of Barton. Use four different colours to identify:

- Hilliard's own thoughts and feelings about Barton
- Barton's action
- dialogue
- physical description of Barton.

b) Summarise in your own words the character of Barton in one or two sentences.

ACTIVITY 5

a) Write a description of a very rude and angry man, Mr Stickles. He is cross with the children who live next door to him because they keep kicking their football over the fence into his garden.

We could hear him in the garden, scraping at some weeds on his patio. It was my turn to stand on a garden chair, look over the fence, and ask, once again, for Mr Stickles to return our ball.

Write some brief dialogue to show how rude Mr Stickles is.

....

....

....

....

....

He walked towards me and I could see, for the first time, what he really looked like.

Write a description of an angry Mr Stickles.

....

....

....

....

With great reluctance, Mr Stickles set off towards our ball. It had, unfortunately, landed right in the middle of his bed of newly planted petunias.

Describe how Mr Stickles picks up the ball and throws it back over the fence.

....

....

....

....

I caught the ball and watched him walk back towards his patio and his small, neat pile of pulled weeds. He stood still for a moment before, yet again, bending awkwardly and slowly towards his task.

Write what the narrator feels and thinks about Mr Stickles.

....

....

....

....

....

ACTIVITY 5

b) Look again at the plan you produced for Activity 2 a). Write a section of your story in which you present a character. Use your responses to Activity 4 a) and b) and Activity 5 a) to help you.

....

....

....

....

....

....

....

....

Describing place

It is often a good idea to write interesting descriptions of a place. This is likely to be towards the beginning of your response, but it could be at other points as well. Writing a description of a place is a good opportunity to use some well-chosen writing techniques such as metaphors.

ACTIVITY 6

a) Look at this extract from the opening of a short story called 'The Fly in the Ointment' by V. S. Pritchett. Annotate the extract to show some of the methods Pritchett uses to describe the setting. Two annotations have been completed for you.

> A short, impactful sentence to establish the time. 'Dead hour' links with the sense of decay in the rest of the passage.

It was the dead hour of a November afternoon. Under the ceiling of level mud-coloured cloud, the latest office buildings of the city stood out alarmingly like new tombstones, among the mass of older buildings. And along the streets the few cars and the few people appeared and disappeared slowly as if they were not following the roadway or the pavement but some inner, personal route. Along the road to the main station, at intervals of two hundred yards or so, unemployed men and one or two beggars were dribbling slowly past the desert of public buildings to the next patch of shop fronts.

> Carefully chosen vocabulary. The verb 'dribbling' suggests the slow, unpleasant movement of the people in the city.

ACTIVITY 6

b) Write a description of a city park on a sunny Saturday afternoon. Begin by describing the park in general (the weather, the warmth of the sun, the trees, the people, the children playing, etc.) before focussing on a dirty, empty park bench in a shaded corner.

Use **at least** one of the following in your description:

- a deliberately short sentence (e.g. 'It was the dead hour of a November afternoon.')
- a carefully chosen verb (e.g. 'dribbling')
- a carefully chosen adjective (e.g. '**dead** hour')
- a simile (e.g. 'the latest office buildings stood out like new tombstones')
- a metaphor (e.g. 'the ceiling of level mud-coloured cloud').

Engaging creative prose writing

In order to achieve a Grade 5, you will need to show that you can engage your reader. You can achieve this by considering the following:

- narrative perspective
- figurative language
- engaging vocabulary.

Narrative perspective

You could choose to write in first person. This is when you present a single viewpoint from the perspective of the person writing the story, using personal pronouns 'I' or 'we'. This may be a sensible choice for tasks that encourage you to write from a personal experience or memory, such as **'Write about a time when you helped somebody'**.

You could choose to write in third person. This allows you to present different people's viewpoints or the thoughts of a single person who is not the person writing the story, using pronouns such as 'they', 'she' or 'he'.

Whichever narrative perspective you choose, **you need to make it the same all the way through your response**.

Figurative language

Figurative language includes methods such as similes, metaphors and personification. They can help your reader imagine the story, characters and setting of your response. They can also help you to establish a mood or atmosphere.

A **simile** is a comparison using 'like' or 'as'. It shows the similarity between two different things. For example, 'The bare trees scraped the grey sky like claws.' This example also helps to establish a menacing atmosphere.

A **metaphor** is a comparison between two different things, where one is described as the other. For example, 'The summer sky is a blue tent to keep out the rain.' This metaphor adds to a contented mood.

Personification is giving human qualities to something which isn't human. For example, 'The disappearing trees seemed to wave goodbye to us in the wind.' This personification helps to suggest a certain sadness.

ACTIVITY 7

a) In the box below, write down what you might see and hear in a city park on a sunny afternoon. For example:

> Ducks in a pond
> People having a picnic

b) Choose something from the box in Activity 7 a). Describe it using a metaphor, a simile or personification. Complete the table below.

Aspect of a city park	Description	Method used
People having a picnic	The multi-coloured picnic rugs bloom like flowers across the lawn.	Simile

Engaging vocabulary

You need to choose your words carefully in order to achieve particular effects and to help make your writing interesting and engaging.

ACTIVITY 8

The extract from a student's response below is limited because the highlighted words have not been carefully chosen.

> The best birthday I ever had was just last year. In the morning, as usual, I took my dog for a walk in the local park. I remember it being particularly busy that day. The weather was good and there was loads of shade. But, as I turned the corner at the far end of the park, I saw something weird: a massive crowd gathering at the edge of the nice pond.

Fill in the gaps with carefully chosen and interesting words or phrases.

The most memorable birthday I ever had was just last year. In the morning, as usual, I took my dog for a walk in the local park. I remember it being particularly busy that day. The weather was _____ and there was _____ of shade. But, as I turned the corner at the far end of the park, I saw something _____: a _____ crowd gathering at the edge of the _____ pond.

Bringing it all together

This chapter has so far covered the following aspects of Grade 5 creative prose writing:

- aspects of narrative (setting, events, character)
- ways to structure a story
- the importance of engaging openings
- effective characterisation
- effective descriptions of place
- narrative perspective (first or third person)
- figurative language
- carefully chosen vocabulary.

A student has started a response to this task: **'Write about a time when you helped somebody.'** The paragraph has many of the hallmarks of a Grade 3 response.

GET GRADE 5

This opening could be more engaging: you could begin with a vivid description, some dialogue, a mystery or an exciting event.

There is an opportunity here for you to describe the setting in interesting and engaging ways.

Can you use some figurative language to describe the scene here?

This word is rather general and could have been more carefully chosen.

You are attempting to convey the character of Amir here. Perhaps describing Amir's actions or physical appearance could help.

I remember a time when I helped somebody. I was with my two younger brothers, Amir and Mohammed, on our way home from school. It was December so it was already getting dark and the weather was bad. It was raining and really windy.

Amir was only eleven and he was moaning about how cold and tired he was. I had to keep telling him to keep up because I wanted to get home quickly myself.

We eventually turned the corner onto Sycamore Road and I saw a parked car. Its hazard warning lights were flashing in the rain. An old woman was standing in the rain looking at a tyre. As I got closer, I could see that the tyre was flat and the woman was looking quite distressed. I was the oldest and, even though we all wanted to get home ourselves, I decided to ask her if she was all right.

ACTIVITY 9

a) It was December so it was already getting dark and the weather was bad. It was raining and really windy.
Re-write this description to make it more interesting.

....

....

....

....

b) Amir was only eleven and he was moaning about how cold and tired he was.
Convey the character of Amir here by adding details of his appearance and actions.

....

....

....

....

....

ACTIVITY 10

The student then responded to the teacher's feedback and wrote the response below. The response is now on course to achieve at least a Grade 5. Read the teacher's annotations to see how the student has improved the response.

You continue with the idea of a battle here with the metaphor of the assault – very creative! The image of the wind slapping your faces is also a very effective way of getting across the extreme weather.

You have made Amir a much more interesting character by including some dialogue and description of his appearance and actions.

I've never really considered myself to be a particularly helpful person. I try to just keep my head down, stay out of trouble and keep myself to myself. There was one day, however, when I helped somebody – and my life was never quite the same again.

It all happened three years ago. I was with my two younger brothers, Amir and Mohammed, on our way home from school. It was December so it was already getting dark and the weather was a horrendous battle. Our coats provided no defence against the rain's assault and the wind seemed to slap our faces.

Amir was only eleven. The evening gloom made him look even smaller and younger. His head was down and his hands were planted firmly in his pockets. He looked up occasionally, but only to moan and complain: 'I'm so cold. Why isn't Mum picking us up?' I just kept telling him to keep up. I wanted to get home quickly myself.

We eventually turned the corner onto Sycamore Road and I saw a parked car. Its hazard warning lights were flashing in the rain. An old woman was standing in the rain looking at a tyre. As I got closer, I could see that the tyre was flat but it was like all the air had come out of the old woman as well. I was the oldest and, even though we all wanted to get home ourselves, I decided to ask her if she was all right.

This is a really interesting opening – you have created a mystery which will make the reader want to read on. There is also an effective use of the rule of three here.

This is much better than 'bad'! You communicate how violent the weather is through this choice of words.

A very effective simile comparing the old lady with a flat tyre.

a) How does this description of the weather and of Amir's character compare with your own?

....
....
....

b) Which is your favourite part of this student's response and why?

....
....
....
....

ACTIVITY (11)

Read the following extracts from student responses to this task: **'The Park Bench'**

A Every lunch I would leave the office to buy a sandwich from the same supermarket. I would then take the sandwich to the same local park. Every day I would sit on the same bench and eat my sandwich. I liked the bench because it was in the shade and there was an amazing view of the park and the hills around the town.

One day I walked to the park with my sandwich in hand and, for the first time in over two years, somebody was sitting on my bench. It was an old man. His hair was grey like wire and he had a walking stick. I didn't know what to do. I didn't know whether I should sit on the same bench next to him or walk to another bench in the hot sun. I decided to sit down next to him.

When I sat down next to him, he looked at me and smiled. He then said something I will never forget …

B I always bought my lunch in the supermarket and walked to the park. I would always sit on the same bench to eat my lunch because I liked the view and it was always in the shade.

One day something different happened. I walked to the park and there was an old man sitting on the bench. He was really old with grey hair.

I sat down next to him. He looked at me and told me something really memorable.

C Let's just say I'm a creature of habit. At 1 p.m. on the dot I always leave the office, walk to the supermarket and buy a cheese and pickle sandwich and a carton of orange juice. At 1.15 p.m. I arrive at the park and sit on my favourite bench. The bench is in a perfect position and is always empty. It seems to wait coolly in the shade in the hot summer months for me to sit on it. From the bench, I can look out across the park and up towards the comforting blanket of rolling hills which surround the town.

One day, however, I walked to the bench and there was somebody sitting on it. Somebody sitting on my bench.

He was bolt upright, like he was sitting to attention. His eyes were bright and alert and, as I approached, I noticed he was looking right at me, like he had been expecting me. Like he knew me.

'Sorry, is it alright if I …?' I mumbled.

He smiled and nodded, never once taking his eyes off me.

I began to eat my cheese and pickle sandwich in silence. After a while, out of the blue, he started talking. And he told me something I will never forget …

ACTIVITY (11)

Match up the responses with the teacher comments below.

Teacher comment 1

This is a straightforward response. You write accurately and communicate your ideas in a structured way. The vocabulary could be more varied. You focus mostly on the events: you could engage your reader further by describing the park or the character of the old man.

Response A ☐
Response B ☐
Response C ☐

Teacher comment 2

You start with an engaging opening which hooks the reader. Your description of the bench and the view is creative with some effective figurative imagery. Your words have been very carefully chosen and your sentences are varied for effect. The man on the bench is conveyed as a really interesting and unusual character and you have structured the response carefully to make the reader want to read on.

Response A ☐
Response B ☐
Response C ☐

Teacher comment 3

You communicate your ideas clearly and sensibly. The response is thoughtfully structured. You attempt some engaging techniques such as patterning in the first paragraph and a simile. You now need to do more of this in an effort to engage and interest your reader.

Response A ☐
Response B ☐
Response C ☐

Extended practice

Complete one of the following four Component 1 creative prose writing tasks. Limit yourself to ten minutes of planning and 35 minutes of writing and checking your response. Remember to consider and apply the skills and approaches covered in this chapter.

You should aim to write about 450–600 words.

Choose **one** of the following titles for your writing:

a) The Theme Park

b) Continue the following: I woke to the unmistakeable sound of an avalanche.

c) Write about a time when you lost something.

d) Write a story which ends: I looked behind me and the dog was no longer there.

CHECK YOUR PROGRESS

You have now practised the skills needed for a Grade 5 response to the creative prose writing task for Component 1. Read through your response to the Extended Practice task.

Tick if you feel the statement applies to your response.

	✔
I planned my response carefully before I began writing.	
I used the suggested structure for a narrative: ■ establish setting and character ■ a complication ■ a development or consequence ■ an ending.	
I engaged my reader in the opening paragraph.	
I conveyed character effectively through thoughts/feelings, dialogue, action and/or physical description.	
I have created an interesting sense of place.	
I have used a range of methods, words and phrases to impact my reader.	
My response clearly matches the task.	
I have written an interesting piece of creative prose writing.	

Your reflections

Reflect on the progress check you completed. Which elements of the creative prose writing task for Component 1 do you feel more confident about? Which areas do you feel you still need to work on?

....

....

....

....

....

Component 2, Section B: Writing

Component 2 writing section: Transactional and persuasive writing

This section of the exam will assess the skill of writing for different purposes and audiences. For example, you may be asked to write an article for a magazine to give your view on the benefit of social media, or you may be asked to write a speech in which you give advice on places to visit in your local area.

There will be **two** writing tasks, and you must complete both of them. The questions are likely to ask you to write an article, formal letter, report, leaflet/guide or speech. You will also be assessed on the accuracy of your grammar, punctuation and spelling (see Chapter 13 in this workbook for ways you can improve the accuracy of your writing).

Each question is worth 20 marks (40 marks in total). You should aim to write about 300–400 words and spend 30 minutes on each question, including at least five minutes on planning and a few minutes to check your response.

Example writing tasks

Remember you need to complete both tasks.

This is reminding you that the examiner is looking at how you adjust your writing to suit the different audiences and purposes.

You are not required to write pages and pages for this task. Up to two pages of clear, well-planned writing is normally sufficient for each task.

A range of different combinations of text types and audiences could come up. Here, you are asked to write an article and a guide. These tasks also specify the intended audience: students and visitors to your local area.

Answer Question 1 **and** Question 2.

Think about the purpose and audience for your writing.

You should aim to write about 300–400 words for each task.

1 Some people think that listening to music while studying helps them to concentrate and makes them work better. Write an article for your school or college magazine in which you give your view on this topic.

2 Write an engaging guide for visitors to your local area, advising them what to see and do.

The purposes of the two tasks will be different. Here, you are asked to give a point of view and to advise.

EXAM TIP

Any audience named by the question will usually mean that you can write formally, for a general reader, rather than having to know about a specific person and their background.

How do I achieve a Grade 5 in my response to this task?

You will need to satisfy the following criteria in order to achieve a Grade 5 for the writing section of Component 2:

- You need to communicate your ideas clearly and effectively.
- Your writing needs to be clearly matched to the relevant form, audience and purpose.
- You need to use individual words, phrases and methods to impact your readers.
- You will need to organise your whole piece of writing, and the paragraphs within it.

You will also need to write accurately by meeting the following criteria:

- Use a range of vocabulary.
- Spell most words correctly, including some complex and sophisticated words.
- Write in correctly punctuated sentences.
- Use a variety of sentences to achieve specific effects.
- Write in **Standard English** – the type of English (for example, spelling, punctuation and grammar) widely accepted as being 'correct'.

Chapter 13 will focus on how to improve the accuracy of your writing.

Reading and understanding the question

Before you start planning and writing your response, you need to read the question carefully. You will need to work out the text type (form), audience and purpose. Use the acronym **TAP** to help you:

- **T**ext type: For example, a report, a letter, a speech, an article.
- **A**udience: This could be teenagers, parents, teachers, local residents. It may be a specific person, such as your head teacher. It may be the general public.
- **P**urpose: You may be asked to express your view on something, so you will be writing to persuade or argue. The purpose may be more transactional, such as writing to recommend, advise, inform or review. Some tasks may be a combination of different purposes.

Completing the activities throughout this chapter will clarify how to write effectively for different text types, audiences and purposes.

ACTIVITY 1

Look at these two examples of writing tasks for Component 2. Identify the **T**ext type, **A**udience and **P**urpose for each one.

a) 'Young people spend too much time indoors.'
Write a speech for a school or college assembly in which you argue your point of view on this statement.

Text type: ....

Audience: ....

Purpose: ....

b) Write a letter to your head teacher explaining how to improve your school or college.

Text type: ....

Audience: ....

Purpose: ....

Writing for a purpose

For the writing section in Component 2 you will need to show you can write effectively for different transactional and persuasive purposes. Transactional writing includes texts that advise, inform or explain.

ACTIVITY (2)

a) Draw a line to match the purpose to the definition.

Argue		Make the case for something.
Persuade		Make clear why or how something works.
Advise		Try to get the reader to do something or to change their mind.
Inform		Help people decide what to do and how to do it.
Explain		Tell a reader about something.

b) Read these extracts from student responses. What do you think each student's purpose is? How do you know? Use the list of purposes in the table above to help you.

i The suffering animals, starved of food and care, desperately need your donations.

Purpose: ....

I know this because: ....

ii If you want to see the delights of the Market Square, you could brave the maze-like one-way system in a car but I recommend you catch the 46 tram which takes you straight to the very centre of town.

Purpose: ....

I know this because: ....

iii There are a number of reasons why this old-fashioned attitude is wrong. Firstly, young people spend much of their time either at school or studying at home and social media is a chance to relax and unwind.

Purpose: ....

I know this because: ....

iv The body does not work in mysterious ways: it is simple science. It will grow and be strong if it is given the right balance of nutrition and a variety of food groups.

Purpose: ....

I know this because: ....

v Our school is just twenty years old. You probably didn't know that it was built in 2001 at a cost of £20 million.

Purpose: ....

I know this because: ....

105

ACTIVITY ③

a) Write a letter to your head teacher explaining how to improve your school or college.

*This task is asking you to **explain** how to improve your college. Write a paragraph in response to this task. Your point should be to suggest improvements to the food served at lunchtime. Remember you are **explaining** what the problem is and how it could be improved.*

....

....

....

....

....

....

....

....

b) Write a letter to your head teacher in which you persuade them to improve your school or college.

*This task is asking you to **persuade** the head teacher to do something. Write a paragraph in response to this task. Your point should be to get the head teacher to change their mind and invest more money in the food served at lunchtime. Remember you are **persuading** the head teacher to do something they are unwilling or unable to do.*

....

....

....

....

....

....

....

....

c) Look again at your responses to Activity 3 a) and b). What would you say are some of the significant differences between the two?

....

....

....

Writing for an audience

In some questions, the audience you are writing for may be clearly stated – such as a local MP. Other questions might suggest an audience: for example, writing for a local newspaper implies a local audience.

Regardless of the specified audience, you need to write in clear, well-organised Standard English. Avoid slang and ensure you use accurate, standard grammar.

You should make sure your writing is directed sensibly towards your specified audience. A speech on social media to fellow classmates should be different from a speech on social media to older people. Acknowledge your audience's possible interests, concerns and priorities.

ACTIVITY 4

Read these two paragraphs, taken from Grade 5 student responses to two different exam tasks. Both students have successfully written their pieces for their different audiences.

Underline and annotate the paragraphs to indicate where and how they are successfully adapting their response for their audience.

> Write a letter to your head teacher in which you persuade them to improve your school or college.

As a Head teacher, you will understand the need to have students at your school who are fresh, alert and full of energy. They will learn more and achieve better grades for your school. Your recent assembly on having a balanced, healthy diet certainly made a lot of sense, but I am afraid the food at the school canteen is a long way from being balanced or healthy. As a result, the students at your school attend their Period 5 lessons after lunch feeling tired and unhealthy from all the fried, greasy food.

> 'Young people spend too much time indoors.'
> Write a speech for a school or college assembly in which you argue your point of view on this statement.

Our teachers here at school work us hard and, after six lessons, we can all feel a bit jaded. I'm sure many of you, like me, therefore enjoy gaming on Xbox, listening to music and messaging friends on social media after a long day at school. But, I ask, are we not at risk of spending too much time on these things? Are we missing out on experiencing the beautiful countryside which surrounds our town, just a few minutes' walk away?

Text types: Articles

You should try to include the following if you are asked to write an article:

- **A headline:** This provides an (often enticing) indication of what the article may be about and what the point of view is.
- **A sub-heading:** This provides more information beneath the headline. Sub-headings can also be used to separate different sections of the article.
- **A lively and engaging style:** To make your readers want to keep reading.

ACTIVITY 5

Look at this extract from an article by Janet Street-Porter in the *Independent*. Underline or highlight the features that are typical of an article.

> **Halloween is nothing more than legitimised begging by aggressive kids in costumes**
>
> *'Celebrities' will be forcing themselves into ludicrous costumes and silly wigs to be photographed by the paparazzi in North London arriving at Jonathan Ross's Halloween party, just like they do every single year. Surely there's an easier way to get your picture in the press?*
>
> Very few things in this life make me anxious or fearful, but next Wednesday is already giving me plenty of concern.
>
> Halloween has become an event feared and loathed by a silent majority who regard it as nothing more than legitimised begging by aggressive kids in silly costumes egged on by pushy mothers. This is a public announcement to all trick-or-treaters in my neighbourhood: I will not be at home, so don't bother turning up and ringing my doorbell like you did last year, on and off for three long hours. My letterbox will be taped up so you can't scream through it.

EXAM TIP

In the exam you do not need to write the headline in large block writing – just use your normal handwriting.

Text types: Letters

You may be asked to write a formal letter. You should try to include the following in a formal letter:

- Your address and date go in the top right-hand corner.
- The person you are writing to and their address goes lower down on the left.
- Use 'Dear Sir/Madam' if you don't know the name.
- Use Mr/Mrs/Ms/Miss if you do know the name.
- It may be appropriate to use a subject line to indicate what the topic of the letter is going to be about (for example, 'Local speed restrictions').
- Sign off with 'Yours faithfully' if you have used 'Dear Sir/Madam'. If you have used the person's name, sign off with 'Yours sincerely'.
- Write your full name beneath the sign off.

EXAM TIP

The most important thing is the quality and accuracy of your writing. Try to include these features of letter writing, but the examiner is much more interested in what it is you actually write in the main body of the letter.

ACTIVITY 6

Write a letter to your head teacher in which you persuade them to improve your school or college.

Practise including the features of a formal letter by writing part of a response to the above task. You do not need to include the main body of the letter for this activity. Use a separate piece of paper.

Text types: Speeches

You should try to include the following if you are asked to write a speech:

- Introduce yourself: 'Good afternoon and thank you for taking the time to listen. My name is Jessica and I'm here to talk about cats. Yes, cats.'
- After you have introduced yourself, make an attention-grabbing opening sentence: 'Climate change will wipe out our civilisation' or 'Homework is a complete waste of time and effort'.
- Think of ways you can address your audience throughout your speech:
  - Ask them questions: 'How many of you get distracted by your phone when you are meant to be doing your homework?'
  - Use the pronouns, 'we' and 'you'.
  - Acknowledge the audience in other ways: 'I can see some of you shaking your head' or 'I'm sure many in the audience will agree'.
- Thank your audience for listening. For example, 'Thank you. Any questions?'; 'Thank you for listening and feel free to check my blog for further information'; 'Thank you all and have a safe journey home'; 'Thank you so much and best of luck for your future careers'.

ACTIVITY 7

Write a **short** speech for college or school assembly in which you explain **one** reason why it is important to have a healthy and active lifestyle.

Try to include some or all of the features of a speech listed above. For this activity, you should try to keep your speech short. You only need to explain **one** reason.

....

....

....

....

....

....

....

....

....

....

Text types: Reports

You should try to include the following if you are asked to write a report:

- The title should be formal and factual.
- Your introduction should provide the main facts about the topic.
- You should then move on to consider the current situation – what is happening now.
- You should then move on to your recommendation – what you feel should change.
- You should then describe the advantages your proposed changes will bring.
- Reports are information texts, but there is still scope for you to provide compelling opinions on the situation and your recommendations.

ACTIVITY 8

On a separate piece of paper, plan or write a response to the following exam-style task:

> You have been asked by the local council to write an informative report on the state of the facilities in your local park. Write the report. Aim for 300 words.

Planning a response

The first part of the process is to read the question carefully and work out the **T**ext type, **A**udience and **P**urpose.

> Some people think that listening to music while studying helps them to concentrate and makes them work better. Write an article for your school or college magazine in which you give your view on this topic.

ACTIVITY 9

What is the **T**ext type, **A**udience and **P**urpose for the task above?

Text type: ....

Audience: ....

Purpose: ....

Some tasks, like the one above, will ask you for your point of view or how far you agree with a statement. Your point of view will need to be clear and in favour of one side or the other.

ACTIVITY 10

Summarise in one sentence your thoughts on whether students should listen to music while studying.

....

....

....

To help you develop your point of view and to generate points for your response, think about all of the different ideas that come to mind when you think about the topic. Think about the benefits of your point of view and how it might solve problems.

ACTIVITY 11

Put a line through 'should' or 'should not' depending on your point of view in Activity 9. Then go on to complete the spider diagram below with at least four points you could make. Think about the benefits of your point of view and how it might solve problems.

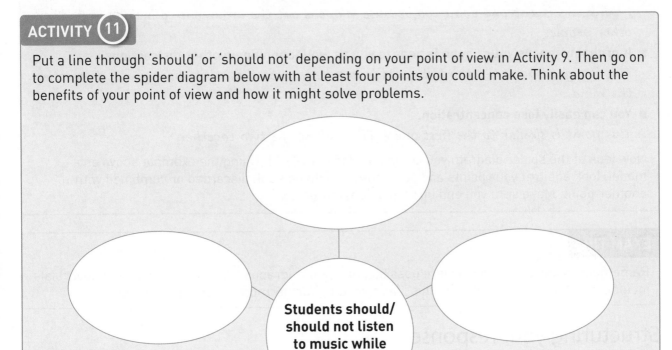

EXAM TIP

Although Activity 11 asks you to use a spider diagram, you could use bullet point planning instead. Experiment with different kinds of plans and settle on the one that you feel most comfortable with.

You should then look again at the points you have come up with. Be prepared to remove some or combine some points together.

ACTIVITY 12

Look at how one student has thought about the points from their original plan.

■ **Music distracts rather than focuses the mind.**
  I like this point on distraction and I can think of examples and evidence to support the point.
■ **It drains the battery on the phone.**
  I'm not sure this point is really relevant and it won't help me to develop my argument – I'll cross this one out.

ACTIVITY (12)

- **You can disturb other people who are studying.**

  I think this is a strong point too because it opens out the argument to include impact on other people.

- **It probably means your phone is near to you as well, opening up other distractions.**

  This is a good point – I think it could link quite well to the point about music distracting the mind.

- **You can easily lose concentration.**

  This point is similar to the first one – I'll combine the two together.

Now look at the spider diagram you completed for Activity 11. Using the example above as a model, look again at your points and see if they should be kept, discarded or combined with another point. Make sure you end up with at least three points.

EXAM TIP

Remember to use adverbials, where possible, to link paragraphs together. Some useful adverbials include 'in addition', 'in relation to this', 'as a result', 'furthermore', 'not only ... but also ...'.

Structuring your response

Once you have generated and selected your ideas, you need to think about the way you can organise these into a well-structured response. An effective way of achieving this is to sequence your ideas logically, so that one point leads to, and is developed by, the next.

> 'Young people spend too much time indoors.'
>
> Write a speech for a school or college assembly in which you argue your point of view on this statement.

Now look at these points that a student noted in a plan written in response to the exam-style task above.

- *You are more likely to meet people and socialise.*
- *Outdoors is good for your health: fresh air, being active.*
- *Being outside is good for the mind– it helps you to relax.*
- *You are more likely to learn and have new experiences outside.*

The student then considered the best way to sequence the points:

1 Outdoors is good for your health: fresh air, being active.

  I think this is a good, strong point to begin with.

2 Being outside is good for the mind – it helps you to relax.

  This is a clear development from the previous point, moving from physical health to mental health.

3 You are more likely to learn and have new experiences outside.

  I can now move from mental health to the general, all round benefits of learning and having new experiences.

4 You are more likely to meet people and socialise.

  Meeting new people could be a clear development from having new experiences; this could also be a powerful point to end on: being around others is better than being on your own.

ACTIVITY 13

Look at the points you selected for Activity 11. Decide now on the best way to structure your points. Use the student comments above to help you. You will need at least three points but you may have more. Complete Column 1 of the table in Activity 14.

It may also be possible at this stage in the planning process to think of ways in which your point could be supported. This could be achieved by including one or more of the following:

- a personal experience (called an **anecdote**)
- a fact or statistic
- an expert's point of view
- other 'real world' examples.

For the first point in the plan – **Outdoors is good for your health: fresh air, being active** – the student thought it this could be supported by a fact or statistic. For example, people who go for regular outdoor walks are less likely to suffer from heart disease in later life.

EXAM TIP

Real life facts and statistics are always preferred. You can make them up, however, if needed, but make sure they are believable.

ACTIVITY 14

Now complete Column 2 with some ideas about how you could support each of the points you are making.

Point	Support for the point

ACTIVITY 14

Point	Support for the point

EXAM TIP

Paragraphing is very important for the Writing section. Make sure that your response presents **one** idea or point **per paragraph**.

This point or idea should be clearly stated in the first sentence of the paragraph, known as the **topic sentence**. The rest of the paragraph should build on this key point.

Writing an effective introduction

An introduction should clearly establish your view and engage the reader's interest. Avoid vague or general statements and do not simply list the points you are going to make in the main body of your response. Your introduction should be short and memorable.

ACTIVITY 15

Write a lively article for a local newspaper with the heading: 'Why we need to switch off our phones every now and then'.

Five students have written an introduction to the task above. Tick those that you feel are effective introductions.

1 Imagine a futuristic world where everybody shuffles, head down, permanently attached to a shiny electronic device. Well, we are living in the future. And the enslaving electronic device is the smart phone. ☐

2 In this article I am going to be explaining that we all need to switch off our phones. ☐

3 There are lots of reasons why we need to switch off our phones: we are in danger of becoming addicted, we are missing out on living in the real world and social media has become a platform for bullying. ☐

4 It is the first thing we look at when we wake up in the morning. It is the last thing we look at when we go to bed at night. Isn't it time we woke up to something else instead — to the stark fact that we are, sadly, all addicted? ☐

ACTIVITY 16

Look again at your plan for Activity 13. Write an introduction below. Remember to:

- include some of the features of a speech (see Activity 7 on page 109)
- clearly establish your point of view
- engage the reader's interest
- keep it short and memorable.

Use some of the examples in Activity 15 to help you.

....

....

....

....

....

....

Using language effectively

Using different language methods can add power and impact to your writing for Component 2. In Chapter 7 of this workbook, you looked at the ways in which writers can make their writing more engaging and persuasive. For the Writing section of Component 2, you need to show you that you can use some of these techniques yourself.

Look at how Janet Street-Porter, the writer of this article, has used language to engage and persuade her readers.

This is an opinion disguised as a fact; it makes her argument stronger and suggests the majority of people agree with her.

The writer might be **exaggerating** in this verb here.

Halloween has become an event feared and loathed by a silent majority who regard it as nothing more than legitimised begging by aggressive kids in silly costumes egged on by pushy mothers. This is a public announcement to all trick-or-treaters in my neighbourhood: I will not be at home, so don't bother turning up and ringing my doorbell like you did last year, on and off for three long hours. My letterbox will be taped up so you can't scream through it. …

Halloween celebrations have got out of hand, so take my advice – disconnect the doorbell, get under the duvet with a torch and a good book or your laptop, and turn off the lights. For a few short hours, you'll be under siege. Then it's over, for another year.

These **adjectives** have been carefully chosen – the writer's opinion on the children and their mothers is made very clear.

The writer has used patterning – the **rule of three** in this case – to make her advice clear and compelling.

The piece ends with a **short sentence** to make the article powerful and memorable.

The **metaphor** of being 'under siege' by the trick-or-treaters confirms the writer's point of view.

ACTIVITY 17

Look again at your plan for Activity 13 and the introduction for Activity 15. Now write the first point of your article. Use Janet Street-Porter's article on Halloween as a model. Carefully choose at least two of the following to include in your response:

- an assertion
- carefully chosen adjectives and/or verbs to make your opinion clear
- exaggeration
- patterning/repetition (for example, rule of three)
- a metaphor or simile
- a short sentence at the end of the paragraph.

....

....

....

....

....

....

....

....

ACTIVITY 18

Your local council has announced it is planning to close down your local youth club. Write a letter to your local newspaper arguing for or against the closure.

a) Read this paragraph taken from a student's response to the above task.

The local youth club provides service to young people. Young people can gather to play sports and games, such as basketball and pool, in a safe environment. They can play safely and get to meet new people and make friends. Teenagers can also learn new skills as well and talk to the people who work there about any problems they might have.

ACTIVITY 18

After receiving feedback, the student reworked the paragraph to at least a Grade 5 standard. Annotate the paragraph to show where the student has successfully made improvements.

> I find it extraordinary that the local council are considering closing this facility. The youth club provides a precious and extremely important service to young people. It is a space for them to gather for sports and games such as basketball, pool and table football. It is a space for them to socialise safely under the guidance of trained youth workers. It is a space for them to meet new people and make new friends, away from the pressures of school. If the youth club closes, where will they go? What will they do? It is a precious diamond in our community and it should not be so readily thrown away.

b) Now write the next paragraph. Make your point on **how the youth club helps the wider community because it keeps teenagers off the street and away from anti-social behaviour**. Use the Grade 5 paragraph above to help you.

....
....
....
....
....
....
....

Extended practice

Complete the following Component 2 writing tasks. Limit yourself to one hour in total – 30 minutes on each task. Remember to carefully plan and structure each of your responses and to consider and apply the skills covered in this chapter.

Answer Question 1 **and** Question 2.

Think about the purpose and audience for your writing.

You should aim to write about 300–400 words for each task.

1 'Celebrities make good role models for young people.'
  You have been asked to contribute to a classroom debate on this topic. Write a speech in which you argue for or against the statement.

2 Write an engaging guide for visitors to your local area, advising them what to see and do.

CHECK YOUR PROGRESS

You have now practised the skills needed for a Grade 5 response to writing tasks for Component 2. Read your responses to the Extended Practice tasks.

Tick the statements which apply to each of your responses.

	Question 1: Speech on celebrities	Question 2: Guide to local area
I read the question carefully and worked out the Text type, Audience and Purpose.		
My response was well-suited to the Text type, Audience and Purpose.		
I planned my response by jotting down ideas and selecting the best three or four points.		
I thought carefully about the best way to structure my response and sequence my points.		
My introduction: ■ included some of the features of the text type ■ clearly established my point of view ■ engaged the reader's interest ■ was short and memorable.		
I used language effectively and deliberately included some relevant techniques, such as exaggeration, patterning, imagery and short sentences.		

Your reflections

Reflect on the progress check you completed. Which elements of the writing tasks for Component 2 do you feel more confident about? Which areas do you feel you still need to work on?

Components 1 and 2: Technical accuracy

Marks for technical accuracy

In your responses to the writing tasks in both Component 1 and Component 2 you will need to show you are able to use a range of different sentences, a wide vocabulary and that your spelling and punctuation is accurate. This is called **technical accuracy**.

The Component 1 writing task is worth 40 marks in total. Twenty-four marks are awarded for the content and organisation of your response. Sixteen marks are awarded for **technical accuracy** (40%).

Each of the two writing tasks for Component 2 are worth 20 marks. Twelve marks are awarded for the content and organisation of your response and eight marks are awarded for **technical accuracy** (40%).

A lot of marks are therefore available for your technical accuracy and you need to ensure you gain as many as possible.

How do I achieve a Grade 5 for my technical accuracy?

You will need to satisfy the following criteria in order to achieve a Grade 5 for your technical accuracy:

- Use a range of vocabulary.
- Write in correctly punctuated sentences.
- Use a range of different sentences to achieve specific effects.
- Spell correctly, including some more complex and sophisticated words.
- Write in Standard English.

Punctuation

Correct punctuation is really important if you want to make your meaning clear. In order to achieve a Grade 5 you need to use a range of punctuation accurately.

Commas

A common error is to use a comma where you should use a full stop or a conjunction such as 'and' or 'because'.

It is really important we all spend more time outdoors, we need to feel the sunshine and wind on our faces. ✗

This sentence contains two separate pieces of information:

It is really important we all spend more time outdoors

+

we need to feel the sunshine and wind on our faces

A comma should not be used to join them together. Sentences should be separated by a full stop or joined by a conjunction.

It is really important we all spend more time outdoors. We need to feel the sunshine and wind on our faces. ✔

Or

It is really important we all spend more time outdoors because we need to feel the sunshine and wind on our faces. ✔

ACTIVITY 1

Which of these sentences are correctly punctuated? Mark them with a tick.

a) Our school should offer more after-school sports clubs because our students need a more active lifestyle. ☐

b) The light in the car park flickered on and off, a cloud covered the moon. ☐

c) Halloween is a terrible American import and trick-or-treating should be banned. ☐

d) We could see a solitary ship in the distance, it was sailing away from us. ☐

e) I kept my head down and tried to avoid the cracks in the pavement. ☐

f) The woods were shadowy, menacing and full of spite. ☐

g) We need more speed restrictions near our school, it is only a matter of time until somebody gets hurt. ☐

h) Incredibly, young people spend 23 hours a week on their phones and tablets. ☐

i) Climate change is something we all need to take responsibility for, we need to cut down on our energy use and recycle much more. ☐

Apostrophes

Students often miss out apostrophes or use them incorrectly.

a) Apostrophes can indicate a missing letter or letters:
- I will → I'll
- let us → let's
- do not → don't.

b) Apostrophes can be used to indicate possession:
- the teacher**'s** car
- the children**'s** play area.

If the word to which you are adding the apostrophe already ends in **s** you can just add the apostrophe after the s:
- the teacher**s'** cars
- both your parent**s'** permission.

EXAM TIP

Abbreviations such as **can't** and **don't** are more informal than the unabbreviated versions. Think about your purpose and audience when deciding which to use when writing for Component 2.

Speech punctuation

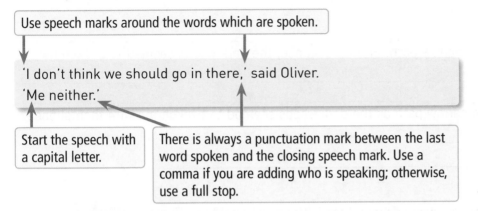

Use speech marks around the words which are spoken.

'I don't think we should go in there,' said Oliver.
'Me neither.'

Start the speech with a capital letter.

There is always a punctuation mark between the last word spoken and the closing speech mark. Use a comma if you are adding who is speaking; otherwise, use a full stop.

EXAM TIP

Avoid too much dialogue in your creative prose writing for Component 1. Writing good dialogue can be very tricky. Also, the examiner wants to see how well you can write full sentences and paragraphs.

Exclamation marks

Be careful when using exclamation marks:

- Never use two or more exclamation marks in a row: 'We need to recycle now!!' ✗
- You should only use an exclamation mark for an actual exclamation, for example, '"How extraordinary!" he cried'. Don't use them randomly throughout your writing or to try to 'liven up' your writing – you need to find other more creative ways of achieving this.

ACTIVITY 2

There are eight punctuation errors in this response. Use the information above on how to punctuate accurately to help you to **identify** and **correct** the errors.

> Harry sat quietly at the back of the classroom. He was trying to make himself as small as possible. Harry watched his teachers eyes, he was desperately hoping she wouldn't pick him.
>
> 'Harry?'
>
> Harry swallowed.
>
> 'Yes miss' he said.
>
> 'Would you like to read out you're story you wrote for homework?'
>
> Theres nothing else to do, Harry thought. He was going to have to make it up as he went along! He walked towards the front of the classroom, he could hear the distant noise of traffic outside, he coughed and scanned the room with his eyes. Then he began to tell his story.

Sentence variety

The examiner is looking for ways in which you vary your sentences in order to alter their impact on the reader. You could, for example, end a paragraph with a very short, powerful sentence. You could choose to put important words or phrases at the beginning or end of a sentence for different effects.

Here are just three ways of including the same words but using a different word order or sentence length:

The dark woods seemed to beckon me from a distance with their silence as I walked anxiously along the narrow path.

Anxiously, I walked along the narrow path. From a distance, the dark woods seemed to beckon me with their silence.

I walked anxiously along the narrow path as the dark woods seemed to beckon me with their silence. From a distance.

ACTIVITY 3

a) Which of the three sentences above do you think is the most effective? Explain your choice.

....

....

....

b) Experiment with at least two different ways of restructuring or resequencing the following sentence. You could break it down into two or more sentences if you wish.

i *I could see my mother waving on the platform as the train approached the station and I immediately knew that she would make all my problems disappear.*

ii ....

....

....

iii ....

....

....

c) Which version do you think is the most effective – i, ii or iii? Explain your choice.

....

....

....

....

EXAM TIP

Short sentences can be particularly effective when they follow a longer sentence or when they appear at the end of a paragraph.

Consistency of tense

In creative prose writing, it is important that your tense remains consistent. It should either all be in past tense or all be in present tense.

Tense is created by the verbs in the sentence:

- I **walked** home and **thought** about my cats. ✔
  These verbs make the sentence past tense.
- I **walk** home and **think** about my cats. ✔
  These verbs make the sentence present tense.
- I **walk** home and **thought** about my cats. ✘
  This sentence is inaccurate because the tense is not consistent. Walk is in present tense and thought is in past tense.

ACTIVITY 4

Underline the verbs in each sentence. Then tick the sentences which use tense consistently.

a) He saw, with horror, the enemy's guns in the distant field and they begin to open fire. ☐

b) The city lights keep the night's darkness away and I think of home. ☐

c) I watch as my teacher walks angrily towards the window. ☐

d) Libby won the match but she thought only of her baby brother. ☐

e) The slugs eat his lettuces while he slept soundly in his bed. ☐

Vocabulary

In order to achieve a Grade 5, you will need to show that you have a varied vocabulary and that you deliberately choose words for the effects they have.

ACTIVITY 5

Consider the effects of these different word choices:

1 The fashion industry **affects** the way teenagers see themselves.
2 The fashion industry **influences** the way teenagers see themselves.
3 The fashion industry **harms** the way teenagers see themselves.
4 The fashion industry **warps** the way teenagers see themselves.

a) What is the difference in effect between sentence 1 and sentence 3?

....

....

b) What is the difference in effect between sentence 3 and sentence 4?

....

....

c) Experiment with two more words with different effects.
- The fashion industry .... the way teenagers see themselves.
- The fashion industry .... the way teenagers see themselves.

EXAM TIP

Don't be afraid to use an effective word because you are not sure about the spelling. The examiner really wants to see how you are using words deliberately to help you to achieve your purposes.

ACTIVITY 6

As Jack desperately clambered up the mountain, he could see the menacing summit force its way through the dark clouds.

As Jack enthusiastically sped up the mountain, he could see the glorious summit peep through the parting clouds.

a) What impression does each sentence create? Which **words** help to create these impressions?

....

....

b) Write a sentence or two describing a boat on an ocean. Try to create a **calm, peaceful effect**.

....

....

c) Now re-write the sentence(s), this time try to create **a sense of danger and threat** by changing some word choices. Use Activity 6 a) to help you.

....

....

ACTIVITY 7

Repeating a word or phrase more than once can make your piece seem uninteresting.

Listening to music while studying clearly has many advantages. Last week, when I was revising for my maths exam, I listened to music. As soon as I put the headphones on, the soothing music helped me to focus on my studies. It does, however, make a difference which type of music I listen to.

a) Which words are repeated in this student's response? Circle them.
b) Re-write the response. Try to avoid repeating these words and phrases by using alternatives.

....

....

....

....

> **EXAM TIP**
>
> It is really important that you leave time at the end of the exam to check your writing. It is easy to make mistakes when writing under timed conditions and checking your work will give you a chance to correct the errors.
>
> Here is a list of common mistakes to look out for when proofreading your work:
>
> - missing punctuation, especially full stops and apostrophes
> - spelling mistakes
> - missing words
> - no paragraphing.
>
> If you forget to start a new paragraph, use **//** to indicate where the new paragraph should begin.

Putting it into practice

Read this Grade 5 response and the accompanying teacher annotations.

> An effective variety of sentences in the opening paragraph. The long second sentence followed by the short final sentence really adds to the effect.

> This short sentence helps to impact the reader and suggest the finality of the broken satnav.

> You have used the full stop accurately here and throughout the response.

> Accurate punctuation of speech.

> This sentence, and the piece as a whole, is consistently in the past tense.

I decided to drive to my brother's new house along the scenic route, away from the grey monotony of the motorway. As I drove deep into the countryside, I could see the golden sun setting through the gaps in the hedgerows and, every now and then, I passed through a pretty village with thatched cottages, an old pub and a church. It was all very beautiful.

Just as the sun set, however, the satnav in my car decided to stop working. Completely kaput. All I could see was a blank screen.

I peered through the windscreen of my car into the threatening darkness. My headlights turned the trees into a ghostly grey colour. And I had no idea where I was. I had no map, no satnav and no sense of direction.

'Just keep going along this road,' I told myself. 'You'll be fine.'

That was the first bad decision I made that night.

> Well-chosen vocabulary to suggest the change in mood from happiness to concern.

> Accurate use of an apostrophe here to indicate missing letters.

125

ACTIVITY 8

The following is a strong response but is at risk of not achieving a Grade 5 because of the errors in technical accuracy. Identify the error in the highlighted sections and write the correct version in the space provided below. The first has been completed for you.

> That morning, like every morning, my mum had to pester me to get me up and ready for school. She started by opening the door loudly before violently flinging open the curtain so the sun shines directly on to my face, I turned around to face the wall.
>
> 'Get up now, Beth' she said. She then waited for a few seconds before repeating: 'Get up now, Beth'
>
> I ignored her. I kept my eyes closed. She yanked my duvet off me. She threw it on the floor.
>
> 'Your going to be late for school, Beth,' she said. Her voice was getting louder. 'Get up now, Beth. I mean it!!'
>
> I slowly opened my eyes. I slowly got out of bed. I picked up the duvet, returned to the bed and pulled the duvet back over me. I closed my eyes and tried to go back to sleep, I hear my mum slam the bedroom door in exasperation.

This should be in past tense: shone.

ACTIVITY 9

This is another strong response but is at risk of not achieving a Grade 5 because of the errors in technical accuracy. Identify and correct the errors.

> Thank you all for coming today and for braving the terrible weather. I'm Freya and I'm here to talk to you about water. Something we all take for granted, especially on days like this. But for some people, waters a rare and precious commodity.
>
> Yehasab lives in a small village in Ethiopia. Twice a day, she has to walk for half an hour to the nearest water source. She has to make the back-breaking journey back to her home. She has to carry 40 litres of water. She has to provide the water for her young family.
>
> But we at Water Relief can help Yehasab and others like her!! We can provide water. Water is a precious commodity, we just need a bit of you're help.

Extended practice

Find your responses to the Extended practice task for the Component 1 writing section on page 86 and/or for the Component 2 writing section on page 103. Alternatively, you could look at any other exam-length responses to a writing task you may have completed in class or at home.

Proofread and correct your response. Pay particular attention to the areas covered in this chapter:

- commas
- apostrophes
- speech punctuation
- exclamation marks
- sentence variety
- consistency of tense
- varied vocabulary
- any other errors you may have made, including spelling and paragraphing.

EXAM TIP

Everybody makes mistakes in their writing, especially under the pressure of timed conditions. You should, therefore, get into the habit of checking your work – both as you go along and when you have finished.

CHECK YOUR PROGRESS

You have now practised the skills needed for a Grade 5 in the technical accuracy of your writing.

Based on the outcome of the Extended practice task above, what would you say are the most common errors you make in your writing?

Why do you think you make these errors more than any others?

Are there any practical steps – such as learning spelling, further practice, checking your work – you can take to reduce the chances of you making these mistakes in the exam?

Sample exam papers

Component 1: 20th century literature reading and creative prose writing

Section A: 40 marks

You are advised to spend ten minutes reading and about 50 minutes answering the questions

Read carefully the passage below. Then answer **all** the questions which follow it.

This passage is taken from a novel called Strange Meeting *by Susan Hill. The novel is partly set in the trenches of the First World War. In this passage, the characters are about to attack the enemy.*

At breakfast, just after six, it was dark and still uncannily quiet. The men's faces were pale, unshaven, their eyes staring. They queued for the bread and rashers of fat bacon, stood or sat about drinking the sweet tea, and there would be nothing to do, once they were in battle order, but stand about again, watching and waiting until their turn came.

5 Walking along towards the platoon sergeant, Hilliard thought that they all knew there was very little chance of this offensive coming off as planned. In simple geographical terms the odds were against them, even though they had confidence in the strength and accuracy of their artillery. Nobody spoke much above a whisper as the dawn came up. But the sky was clear, pale as a dove's back, there had been no more rain. Between the trees of Barmelle Wood half a mile away on the ridge, a thin mist parted and for

10 a few moments the November sun came out, so that the morning frost shone silver-white and the whole landscape seemed to spread and thin out and fade in a trick of light.

Holding the hot tin mug of tea, Barton looked up and saw it all and felt suddenly elated; his muscles were stiff from the few cold hours sleep, he had had a nightmare for the first time since coming to France, full of images of dark green water in which he was drowning, yet now, the knot in his stomach dissolved, he

15 was no longer afraid. He thought of Parkin a few hours before, looked along the line and remembered the hours of work that had gone into the planning of this battle, of the weight of gunpowder and manpower behind them, and thought, we can do it, we can do it, Parkin was right, what is there to be afraid of? And the sun has come out, we are in luck. We must be in luck.

He had a vision of them all going over the top of the trench and running forward up the slope, hundreds

20 and hundreds of them.

'All right?' Hilliard had come back and was standing for a moment beside him. He looked puzzled.

'Yes. I really am.' For he left it, he had the hallucinatory sense of possessing more than one man's share of strength and confidence and hope. *It will be all right.*

'Good.'

25 'Look …' Barton nodded up towards the slop and the wood, to where they could just see Queronne in the lemon-white light.

'It's like a **Turner** canvas.'

Hilliard frowned.

'No – it is. The sun won't last but it won't rain either, and just for now it's very beautiful. Can't you see

30 that?'

'I can see that.'

'What's the matter?'

'You.'

'No, no, I'm fine. I haven't felt like this for weeks. Don't worry about me. You must never worry about me
35   again.'

Filled with unease, Hilliard turned away.

A few minutes later the men took up their places all along the trench. At eight, with a roar like the
explosion of a volcano, the barrage began from their artillery. The men reeled with the shock of the noise
after what had been such an unnaturally long silence. But then, for some time there was a sense of
40   general excitement as they watched the smoke begin to rise up in the direction of the enemy front line,
saw the great flashes of flame and fountains of earth as the guns scored direct hits.

Half an hour later the Rifle Brigade on the left flank came out and began to advance in perfect order. As
far as Hilliard could see the plain in front of the slope was filled with men, following the barrage, sweeping
on without meeting any answering fire. He felt a surge of hope in spite of himself that it was going to
45   work after all, the Surprise Element, that this would be the breakthrough, they would go up the slope and
breach the wood, take over the trenches and gun positions before the Germans had recovered from the
bombardment, which was now the strongest he had ever known. He looked at his watch. He wanted to
go, to have it over with.

The Rifles were still advancing. They were beautiful, Barton thought, standing a dozen yards away behind
50   Private Flannery, they are perfectly ordered, lines unbroken, graceful as horses. They are beautiful.

As the noise of the artillery got louder his excitement seemed to fill his body, took him over entirely so
that, when they themselves began to go up and over the top, he was no longer conscious of anything
except the urge to move forward, to keep up this almost hysterical sense of pleasure in what was so
obviously a perfect battle, so easy, so effortless. He felt as though he were standing outside himself, and
55   was surprised at this new person he had become, surprised at everything. He wondered when he would
come to.

Where the ground began to slope up the mud gave way to grass here and there. But they could no
longer see the men on the right and left flanks because of the denseness of the smoke. Hilliard was
separated from Barton and not so far ahead, so that when the rifle and machine gun fire opened up from
60   the enemy guns hidden in Barmelle Wood, he had a better view. He watched their own first line stagger
and fall, the men going down one after another on their knees and then, before the smoke closed up,
the line immediately behind. It went on like that and after a moment they themselves were caught up in
it, and the heavy shells began to come over, the whole division was an open target for the enemy guns.
Wave after wave of men came walking into the fire, the ground began to open under their feet, as the
65   **howitzers** blew up dozens of men at a time.

Hilliard began to try and pull his own section of the line together, as the men fell he began shouting at
them to close in, before an attack of coughing from the smoke and fumes forced him to stop, gasping for
breath. Four men ahead of him and O'Connor on his right went down in the same burst of machine gun
fire and he wondered how it had missed him so neatly. He went on.

70   After that he lost touch, the men coming up behind overtook his own section and fell in the same places,
so that the bodies were piling on top of one another, the shell holes were filled and then new ones
opened up, filled again. Once, Hilliard slipped and fell and for a moment thought that he had been hit, but
he could feel no pain. A Corporal beside him was holding his head between his hands, covering his eyes
and rocking silently to and fro.

Turner: J. M. W. Turner (1775–1851), an artist known for his painting of sunlight

howitzers: a type of artillery

1 Read lines 1–4. List five things you learn about the men in these lines. [5]

2 Read lines 5–18 What impressions do you get of Hilliard and Barton in these lines?
You must refer to the language used in the text to support your answer, using relevant subject terminology where appropriate. [5]

3 Read lines 19–41. How does the writer show the soldiers' reactions to and preparations for the forthcoming battle?
You should write about:

■ what Hilliard Barton and the other soldiers do, think and say

■ the writer's use of language and structure.
You must refer to the text to support your answer, using relevant subject terminology where appropriate. [10]

4 Read lines 42–56. How does the writer describe the battle in these lines?
You should write about:

■ how different characters respond to the battle

■ what happens

■ the writer's use of language to describe the battle. [10]

5 Read lines 57 to the end. 'In these lines, the writer is showing the real horror of the war.'
How far do you agree with this view?
You should write about:

■ your own thoughts and feelings on how war is presented here and in the passage as a whole

■ how the writer has created these thoughts and feelings.
You must refer to the text to support your answer. [10]

Section B: 40 marks

You should aim to write about 450–600 words. You should spend about ten minutes planning and about 35 minutes writing.

Choose **one** of the following ideas for your writing:

Either:

a) Continue the following: Nobody believed me.

Or

b) Write a text entitled 'My neighbour'.

Or

c) Write about a time when you were told a secret.

Or

d) Write a story which ends: School Sports Day was never quite the same again.

Component 2: 19th and 21st century non-fiction reading and transactional/persuasive writing

Section A: 40 marks

You are advised to spend about ten minutes reading and 50 minutes answering the questions.

Read carefully Source A **and** Source B below. Then answer all the questions which follow.

Source A

This passage is from a biography of Stuart Shorter, a homeless man. The book is called Stuart: A Life Backwards *and it is written by Alexander Masters. The passage begins with Stuart's mother telling Masters about her son's childhood. Stuart has muscular dystrophy, a disease which leads to the weakening of the muscles.*

'Stuart was a happy little boy. A real happy-go-lucky little thing.'

His mother says this was the way he started. Each time we meet, she gives one of her respiratory laughs, leans back in her chair or sofa, puts on a faraway expression, lights another Benson & Hedges, and repeats: 'Yes, a happy, lively little lad. Always up, building things. Absolutely loved it. Anything that he could build he used to like. He'd sit for hours on his own, playing cars and building roads in the dust and the dirt. Yes, quite amazing really.'

Each school morning he waddled, something like a goose, from his parents' house to his classes, half a mile into the village along the country lane and up a short, steep hill, satchel swinging, hand in hand with his brother, to Midston Primary, a skinny, chipper fellow, pleased with the world and with himself. His favourite subjects were battering the water as if it had done him a disservice and calling it 'crawl stroke'; making fat, greasy marks on pieces of paper with coloured crayon, calling them 'Mum'; and sums.

Stuart was talkative, curious, loud, irresponsible, restless, fond of practical jokes, enthusiastic, determined, even wilful, unusually attentive to other people's changes in mood and overfond of embroidering stories. He made friends easily. But despite Stuart's suitability for the school, the headmaster soon noticed something was amiss with the little barmaid's boy. It wasn't just his funny gait: he couldn't kick a football – when he tried he usually missed, coiled up like a rope, pulled a funny face and fell on his nose. He had trouble with steps, too, and no school on a hill could be expected not to have at least a few hundred steps. Slopes were fine. Stuart had got to the school quite happily. It was steps. The sudden up-down, rather than the teeth-gritting push forward. Even the three steps into the front classroom seemed like pitting a boy, a very skinny boy, against a mountain. Stuart had to haul himself up by the banister like a fairground tug-of-war strongman.

Then, one day, Stuart overreached himself in gym. In a fit of exuberance, he shinnied halfway up a rope, lost his grip, fell to the ground and bit through his tongue. Another boy was sent running up to his mother's house.

Stuart was dying.

His spine was smashed up.

His arms and legs were splattered over the wall bars.

When Stuart's mother finally reached the sanitorium, Stuart was sitting in a plastic chair in the corridor, perfectly calm and essentially unharmed. He was not even crying. Indeed, the PE teacher, who agreed that ropes and five-year-old boys have an unhappy tendency to part company sooner than they should, told her that after the initial shock he had not cried at all. His face was covered in drying blood, that was all. He did not need to go to hospital.

131

But it was the final straw for the education authorities. They had seen an ill boy from the start and they weren't about to give up their disquiet just because he could take a tumble as well as the next kid. He had tumbled, that was what mattered. The boy was not fit to be with normal children. They had Stuart transferred to a school for the severely disabled.

sanitorium: a medical facility (in Stuart's school)

Source B

This extract is taken from The Life of Charlotte Brontë (1857), a biography of the writer Charlotte Brontë by Elizabeth Gaskell. The passage describes the boarding school (and local church) in Cowan Bridge that Charlotte attended with her sisters. The passage also describes the treatment of Charlotte's older sister, Maria Brontë.

The path from Cowan Bridge to Tunstall Church, where **Mr. Wilson** preached, and where they all attended on the Sunday, is more than two miles in length, and goes sweeping along the rise and fall of the unsheltered country, in a way to make it a fresh and exhilarating walk in summer, but a bitter cold one in winter, especially to children like the delicate little Brontës, whose thin blood flowed languidly in consequence of their feeble appetites rejecting the food prepared for them, and thus inducing a half-starved condition. The church was not warmed, there being no means for this purpose. It stands in the midst of fields, and the damp mist must have gathered round the walls, and crept in at the windows. The girls took their cold dinner with them, and ate it between the services, in a chamber over the entrance, opening out of the former galleries. The arrangements for this day were peculiarly trying to delicate children, particularly to those who were spiritless and longing for home, as poor Maria Brontë must have been; for her ill health was increasing, and the old cough, the remains of the hooping-cough, lingered about her.

She was far superior in mind to any of her play-fellows and companions, and was lonely amongst them from that very cause; and yet she had faults so annoying that she was in constant disgrace with her teachers, and an object of merciless dislike to one of them, who is depicted as 'Miss Scatcherd' in *Jane Eyre*, and whose real name I will be merciful enough not to disclose …

One of their fellow pupils, among other statements even worse, gives me the following:– The dormitory in which Maria slept was a long room, holding a row of narrow little beds on each side, occupied by the pupils; and at the end of this dormitory there was a small bed-chamber opening out of it, appropriated to the use of Miss Scatcherd. Maria's bed stood nearest to the door of this room. One morning, after she had become so seriously unwell as to have had a blister applied to her side (the sore from which was not perfectly healed), when the getting-up bell was heard, poor Maria moaned out that she was so ill, so very ill, she wished she might stop in bed; and some of the girls urged her to do so, and said they would explain it all to Miss Temple, the superintendent. But Miss Scatcherd was close at hand, and her anger would have to be faced before Miss Temple's kind thoughtfulness could interfere; so the sick child began to dress, shivering with cold, as, without leaving her bed, she slowly put on her black **worsted** stockings over her thin white legs (my informant spoke as if she saw it yet, and her whole face flushed out undying indignation). Just then, Miss Scatcherd issued from her room, and, without asking for a word of explanation from the sick and frightened girl, she took her by the arm, on the side to which the blister had been applied, and by one vigorous movement whirled her out into the middle of the floor, abusing her all the time for dirty and untidy habits. There she left her. My informant says, Maria hardly spoke, except to beg some of the more indignant girls to be calm; but, in slow, trembling movements, with many a pause, she went downstairs at last, – and was punished for being late.

Mr Wilson: a vicar and the owner of the school

Jane Eyre: a novel by Charlotte Bronte; Miss Scatcherd is an unpleasant teacher in *Jane Eyre* and the writer uses this name to refer to the real teacher at the school

worsted: a type of woollen fabric

Read Source A, the extract from the biography *Stuart: A Life Backwards* by Alexander Masters.

1 a) How far away from the village was Stuart's parents' house? [1]

   b) How did the headmaster notice something was wrong with Stuart? Give **one** answer. [1]

   c) Upon hearing of Stuart's fall, what did the education authorities do? [1]

2 How does the writer, Alexander Masters, describe what Stuart was like as a boy?

You should comment on:

■ what the writer says

■ the writer's use of language, tone and structure. [10]

To answer the following questions you will need to read Source B, the extract from the biography of Charlotte Brontë.

3 a) How long is the path from Cowan Bridge to Tunstall Church? [1]

   b) Give **one** detail from the text that suggests the church is an unpleasant place for the children. [1]

   c) Why did Maria want to stay in bed? [1]

4 'The writer, Elizabeth Gaskell, gets across her criticisms of the school really well.'
How far do you agree with this statement?

You should comment on:

■ what she says

■ how she says it.
You must refer to the text to support your comments. [10]

To answer the following questions you must use both texts.

5 Using information from both texts, explain how Maria and Stuart experience school. [4]

6 Both of these texts are about schools.

Compare:

■ what the writers say about the schools

■ how the writers get across their attitudes to their readers. [10]

Section B: 40 marks

Think about the purpose and audience for your writing.

You should aim to write about 300–400 words for each task.

Answer **both** questions.

1 'Schools can be cruel and uncaring places.'

Write a speech for a school or college assembly in which you argue for or against this statement. [20]

2 Your local council is looking for ways to improve the parks in your local area.
Write a report for the council suggesting ways this might be done. [20]

Acknowledgements

The Publishers would like to thank the following for permission to reproduce copyright material.

Pages 9–10: *Stardust* by Neil Gaiman. Reproduced by permission of Headline Publishing Group. © 1999 Neil Gaiman.

Page 10: *From the City, From the Plough* by Alexander Baron. Published by Jonathan Cape (Penguin Random House). Reprinted by permission of The Random House Group Limited. © Alexander Baron 1948.

Pages 12, 94: 'The Fly in the Ointment', from *The complete short stories* by Victor Sawdon Pritchett. Published by Chatto & Windus. Reprinted by permission of The Random House Group Limited. © 1990

Pages 11, 14–15, 19: *The Silent Companions* by Laura Purcell. © Laura Purcell, 2017, *The Silent Companions*, Bloomsbury Publishing Plc.

Pages 20–21, 23, 37: *Small Island* by Andrea Levy. Reproduced by permission of Headline Publishing Group. © 2004 Andrea Levy.

Pages 27, 92, 128–129: *Strange Meeting* by Susan Hill, published by Penguin Books. © Susan Hill 1971, 1989. Reproduced by permission of Sheil Land Associates Ltd.

Page 31: 'The Homecoming' by Milly Jafta. From *Opening Spaces: An Anthology of Contemporary African Women's Writing*, ed. Yvonne Vera, published by Heineman Educational Publishers/Baobab Books. © Milly Jafta 1999.

Pages 32, 33: *The Fifth Child* by Doris Lessing. Reprinted by permission of HarperCollins Publishers Ltd. © Doris Lessing 1988.

Pages 40, 52: *The Wild Places* by Robert Macfarlane. Reprinted by permission of Granta Books. © Robert Macfarlane 2007.

Pages 46, 52, 131–132: *Stuart: A Life Backwards* by Alexander Masters. Reprinted by permission of HarperCollins Publishers Ltd. © Alexander Masters 2005.

Pages 49, 53: 'Peppa Pig: how the ham-fisted cartoon butchered its charm' by Rich Pelley published on 24 Sep 2018. https://www.theguardian.com/tv-and-radio/2018/sep/24/peppa-pig-how-the-ham-fisted-cartoon-butchered-its-charm. Used with permission from Guardian News & Media Limited.

Pages 54–55, 108, 115: 'Halloween is nothing more than legitimised begging by aggressive kids in costumes – I can't stand it' by Janet Street-Porter, published in The Independant on 26 October 2018. Independent article, https://www.independent.co.uk/voices/halloween-costumes-kids-stay-away-pushy-parents-scary-begging-a8603226.html. Used with permission.

Pages 64–65: 'Tips to help your child to take medicine'. Reproduced with permission of Oxford University Hospitals NHS Foundation Trust from its leaflet entitled 'Tips to help your child to take medicine' June 2015, available here: https://www.ouh.nhs.uk/patient-guide/leaflets/files/11990Pmedicine.pdf

Pages 68–69: 'A working life: The lifeboat volunteer' by Mark King. Published on 17 Jul 2010, https://www.theguardian.com/money/2010/jul/17/lifeboat-volunteer-working-life. Used with permission from Guardian News & Media Limited.

Page 72: *Dark Star Safari: Overland from Cairo to Cape Town* by Paul Theroux. Penguin Books 2003. © Cape Cod Scriveners Co., 2002.

Page 84: *A Prison Diary* by Jeffrey Archer. Reproduced with the permission of the Licensor through PLSclear. © Jeffrey Archer 2002.